The Child Millionaire

The Child Millionaire

AN UNCOMMON INVESTMENT GUIDE TO MAKING
YOUR CHILD RICH IN 4 HOURS PER YEAR

Rob West

IGNITION BOOKS

LONDON

Ignition Books is an imprint of Ignition Digital Media.

Published by Ignition Digital Media

For more information on Ignition Digital Media and Ignition Books see www.ignitiondigitalmedia.com and www.childmillionaire.com or email ignitionpublisher@gmail.com

Ignition Digital Media and Ignition Books see publishing as a tool for positive change in the world. We are committed to high quality, action-oriented publishing for people who want to steer their own ship and make life happen. Our overarching objectives are to contribute to a positive, sustainable future. Our mission and sustainability objectives are outlined at www.ignitiondigitalmedia.com. We welcome your feedback and suggestions for future publications.

ISBN: 978-1-908361-03-5

Typeset by Way Out There, London, UK
Cover design by Way Out There, London, UK

Investment/Personal Finance

Contents

Legal Disclaimer vi
Preface viii
Introduction ix

Everything You Need to Know About Investing 1

The Power of Dividends – Getting Paid to be an Owner 9

Market Volatility – Why Market Crashes are Good 18

Inflation and Risk – Why Doing Nothing is Dangerous 25

How to Setup a Child Millionaire Portfolio 34

Investing with ETFs – The Cheap (and Lazy) Answer 41

Investing in Individual Company Shares 53

DRIPing Your Way to a Child Millionaire 60

Ownership and Tax 65

Teaching Your Child about Investing 71

Afterword 74
Resources 75

Legal Disclaimer

You Must Read and Agree to this before Proceeding

The methods outlined in this publication are intended to provide general guidance but not specific advice on how you might set up a very long term investment portfolio for your child.

I am not a professional with respect to investing, financial planning, income tax or investment and tax law, and I am not regulated by any investment or securities authority. The examples I provide in this publication are simply hypothetical examples intended to illustrate general concepts and they are not intended to indicate or quantify levels of risk nor future returns or what you might earn on your money if you follow the examples or principles in the book.

Before undertaking any of the strategies or methods outlined in this publication you should seek appropriate independent expert financial, tax and legal advice relevant to your situation and jurisdiction.

I am not responsible for the completeness, timeliness, validity or legality of any information contained in any website or publication referenced in this publication, so you should verify any information before acting on it.

For full disclosure, I own shares in some of the companies mentioned in this publication. Discussion of any companies or exchange traded funds in this publication is for informational purposes only and does not constitute advice to purchase any securities.

You should understand that investing is inherently risky and you may lose some or all of your capital by investing in any stock/share or other security. The discussion of risk in this publication is only to outline general principles and should not be taken to be comprehensive or authoritative, nor as a basis upon which to make investment decisions. Forecasts and past performance are not reliable indicators of future performance. Shares and other securities are by their nature speculative and can be volatile; you should never invest more than you can safely afford to lose. Information in this publication is for general information only and is not intended to be relied upon by individual readers in making (or not making) specific investment decisions.

Neither I nor the publisher shall have neither liability nor responsibility to any person or legal entity with respect to any financial or other loss or hardship, real or perceived, alleged to have been caused by information in this publication. By reading this disclaimer you agree to accept the conditions contained within it and accept total and complete responsibility and liability for any actions you take based on the information contained within this publication. If you do not wish to agree to and be bound by any or all of these conditions then do not read this publication – instead you may return it to the publisher for a full no-questions-asked refund.

You have been warned, so proceed entirely at your own risk.

Preface

So you want to mint a 'Child Millionaire'...

What follows is a near-foolproof investment method developed over a decade and a half of investing failure, and then profound success. What I've learned and what I am about to impart on you is the result of learning the hard way, which will allow you do it the smart, easy way. In the pages that follow I'll explain a clear and simple system to turn your child into a Child Millionaire with the least possible effort on your part. The system is designed to be setup in mere hours and once setup you can put it almost entirely on autopilot. At most it will require a few hours per *year* to manage, and you only need the basic skills of addition, multiplication and division.

A Few Notes on Countries and Units

I've lived in different countries and travelled to dozens more, and I've written this book broadly with the parents of 'Western' countries in mind. The ideas and methods are transferable pretty much anywhere, but I tend to use examples from the United Kingdom, Canada and the United States as I'm most familiar with these countries and how their investment markets work. Throughout the book you will see me jump between dollars (think US, Canadian, Australian, Kiwi or whatever your dollar is) and British pounds. When I use a $ sign if you live in the UK, simply replace it mentally with a £. The same goes for terminology, which is slightly different in different countries; for example a 'mutual fund' in the US or Canada is usually called a 'unit trust' in the UK; and 'stock' or 'stock market' is the same as 'share' or 'share market'. I'll also give examples from different places and make references to different tax systems. Remember, the point of the Child Millionaire system is principles, which are universal, not the unit of currency or terminology.

Introduction

Going Back to the 80s – or Why You Need to Find $1,000

Imagine it's January 1980 all over again. Perhaps you were born that year and as your parents whisked you home from the hospital (probably without a child car seat or even seatbelts) they stopped in to see their stockbroker, handed over some money they'd saved for you and asked him to buy $1,000 (about $3,000 in today's money) worth of shares in Johnson & Johnson (J&J) and to reinvest the dividends. They then took you home, forgot about the $1,000, and got stuck into their busy new life as parents, consuming along the way considerable amounts of Johnson & Johnson products such as baby powder, baby shampoo and skin lotion.

It's now January 2011. You have a new child of your own born just last week, and on your 31st birthday your parents give you a card. Inside is a statement showing that you own shares in J&J that your parents bought for you and that you didn't even know about. The statement runs to many, many pages showing dividend payments and share purchases with these dividends for every quarter for 31 years. The statement records an initial $1,000 investment, which bought 14 shares, and way down at the bottom it shows the current value: 1,295 shares worth $78,556.43 and earning you dividend income this year of $2799.36. Your parents' half-hour stop in at the stockbroker on the way home from the hospital has provided a return of 7,755.64% on their money and they didn't have to lift a finger. It is a very happy birthday indeed.

With a new child of your own, you now decide not to spend any of the money but rather to keep the plan going and give it to your child. However, it's expensive being a parent and, since you are too strapped for cash to contribute anything else to the portfolio, you just file the statements and leave it. Meanwhile, J&J continues selling baby powder and shampoo, but now there are lots more people in Asia and Latin America buying it.

It's now January 2029. You are 49, and it's your daughter's 18th birthday. She's quite artistic, and she drops the bombshell that she wants to go to art school and become a sculptor. A typical parent, perhaps your own, may have needed a sedative. An artist! Visions of a life of student housing, flipping burgers and destitute grandchildren – why not something practical and career-oriented like computer programming, accounting, law or engineering? Not you though. With a smile of encouragement you hand her a birthday card. In it is the J&J statement. A lot of shampoo has been rinsed down the drain since 1980. The bottom line now reads: 7,575 shares worth $2.23 million and earning $237,000 per year in dividend income. When she gets out of art school in four years this will have ballooned to almost $5.5 million and her income will be over $600,000 a year. By the time she turns 29, some 60 years since your parents' trip home from the hospital, and you see your first grandchild, the J&J statement reads somewhere in the region of $30 million and your sculptor daughter has a dividend income stream of over *$4 million per year*. And all this cost was that initial $1,000.

Now you might think this example to be fanciful or far-fetched. Indeed I have taken the liberty of not accounting for income tax (I will get to that later). However what is most remarkable about this story is how easily it could be your story.

The figures above for Johnson & Johnson from Jan 1980–Jan 2011 are in fact the real historical numbers. The numbers beyond 2011 are simply a straightforward projection of the rates of dividend growth, share appreciation and cumulative return that J&J shares experienced for the previous 31 years. Nothing more, and nothing less. And it's not just Johnson & Johnson, though they are well worth considering for your portfolio; I could have used a number of other companies in the US, Canada, the UK, Europe or elsewhere.

So $1,000 turns into *$30 million*. A little bit of money and *a lot of time* means that every child is a 'time millionaire' if, but only if, parents take action. Unlocking this potential is what this book is about. I'm going to show you how to build a Child Millionaire portfolio with no prior knowledge or investment skill in only a few hours.

Before you protest, not having the money is not a valid excuse. Almost anyone can come up with a couple of thousand, be it gifts from parents and grandparents, government baby bonuses or tax credits, selling unwanted stuff on eBay, not buying a coffee on the way to work for one year, not smoking for a couple of months, taking the bus instead of driving, or a little bit of each of these. Or if you really can't scrape the money together, I'll show you how $100, $50 or even $25 a month a can get you started down the road to having a Child Millionaire. With the Child Millionaire system time is more valuable than money, so no matter how little money you have *you must get started now*.

If it's as easy as I claim you might be wondering why everyone isn't creating a Child Millionaire and why is there a whole industry of financial experts out there taking your money and pretending investing is difficult. I'll talk a bit more about this later but suffice to say most people aren't doing this simply because of a *failure to take action* out of a lack of knowledge (this book will help there) or laziness (might even help you here), egged on by experts in the financial industry who are in the business of making investing look complicated to justify their fees. I'll repeat this again – read this book and take action now, and get started while time is on your child's side.

How *Not* to Invest

Before we get into explaining the secrets of the system and how you can build a Child Millionaire portfolio, I'd like to tell you some of my story and the hard lessons I learned so you can benefit from my mistakes.

The Dark Days

I began investing in the early 1990s, when I was a university student, by contributing $50 a month into an investment account I had at my bank. I devoured various books on investing and learned about mutual funds, which were all the rage at the time.

Mutual funds (similar to unit trusts in the UK) are basically pools of money managed by banks or investment companies that purchase different types of investment 'instruments' or 'securities' such as stocks (also known as 'shares'), government and corporate bonds, mortgages, and sometimes more esoteric instruments. In North America, the mutual fund industry is massive, the marketing is relentless and investing is as easy as sending an email. What I didn't realize at the time was how expensive management fees on mutual funds affect your return and, most importantly, why you should trust yourself rather than the 'experts.'

By the late 1990s, I had saved and invested about $4,500, which had been transformed into a 'fortune' of over $13,000 largely because I happened, on the advice of a financial planner, to have invested in one particular mutual fund that invested in internet and communications technology. As global stock markets soared on the 'dotcom' tech boom, my investments tripled in a matter of months. Sadly, like countless others, I confused blind luck and a stock market bubble with being clever.

In August 2000, after the technology-heavy NASDAQ stock exchange was already months past its peak (fools always come late to the party), I withdrew all of my money from mutual funds and threw it into shares of skyrocketing tech companies including, shares of Nortel Networks, one of the darlings of the technology bubble. I was to learn very quickly that randomly throwing money at shares and hoping they go up in value is 'speculating,' not 'investing'. Thinking I was about to score big and be able to pay off my $8,000 student loan and maybe even set me and my wife up for life, I borrowed or 'leveraged' $16,000 on two lines of credit. I used this money to buy an array of shares in Nortel and other technology companies, following the advice of a fee-based subscription investing service. This 'expert' advice, which I'd come across reading a book on the so-called 'new era' of internet and technology investing, set me back $500, a cost I felt was insignificant in light of the serious money I'd soon be making.

The fee-based subscription investment system I purchased was based on the idea that internet and high-tech companies – so-called 'new economy' companies – were part of a 'new economic paradigm.' These 'new economy' companies, I was told, were different from traditional 'old economy' companies that sold tangible products such as cars, oil or cleaning products. New economy companies, so went the storyline swallowed by me and millions of others, were 'leveraging' the then-new power of the internet to leapfrog old economy companies and redefine economics itself. It was a compelling story, and the incredible stock market value of companies seemed to provide the evidence that a new paradigm really had dawned, which spurred on people like me to dump their life savings into these very same companies, driving their values ever higher.

Of course it was all a sham. So-called 'new economy' companies that produced nothing but the promise of a high-tech fantasy were in fact subject to the same fundamental economic laws of gravity as the old economy companies that actually produced things that people needed. So when the tech bubble finally popped it really exploded. The technology-heavy NASDAQ stock market index went from an all-time high of 5,132 on 10 March 2000 to 1,840 in March 2001, a drop of 64% in 12 months. By Sept 2002 the index was below 1,200 and investors had lost *$5 trillion* in the dotcom meltdown.

During the bust, Nortel Networks went from an August 2000 share price of C$124.50 on the Toronto Stock Exchange (TSX) where it comprised a staggering 36.5% of the *entire stock market index* and a market value of C$398 billion, making it one of the highest valued companies in the world, to C$0.47 per share and a market value of C$5 billion by August 2002. Have a look at the peak and crash on the Nortel stock on Yahoo or MSN Finance.

Why didn't I get out before I lost it all? Well, the drop was so rapid that millions of investors, me included, were stunned into inaction, paralysed by the unthinkable. We saw the initial drops of $15 to $20 on a 'bellwether' share like Nortel as minor blips – perhaps even a buying opportunity for us clever, savvy investors to 'double down' before the next big upward run. But in the end it was a catastrophic tidal wave that sank Nortel and hundreds, perhaps thousands, of other tech companies, and millions of people's retirement funds were obliterated.

When the dust settled for me in January 2001, I had lost $15,500 in borrowed money and all but $4,300 of my original pool of capital. My total losses in about 6 months were $24,200, of which $15,500 was money I didn't own and was paying interest on. At the time I was only working part time and earning about $1,800 per month, so the situation was dire. To make payments on the debt I eventually withdrew the remaining $4,300 from my registered retirement fund, paying a tax penalty in the process, and used it to pay down part of the debt, leaving me with $0 savings and $11,500 in debt on my lines of credit, and another $8,000 in student loans. My net worth had gone from $5,000 – my $13,000 investment portfolio minus $8,000 in student loans – to *negative* $19,500 in 6 months. In effect I had more than *twice* the debt as when I graduated from university nine years earlier. I'd been steamrolled by the markets, pulverized by stupidity and annihilated by blind reliance on so-called 'experts' spinning a tale of gold.

The Sunny Days

Fast forward 10 years to early 2011 and the world is a very different place. During the past decade, my wife and I moved to London, paid off all debts, created a robust investment portfolio using many of the methods I'll explain shortly and we've managed to travel to 40 countries. In fact in late 2010, we finished a 14 month round-the-world trip financed by investments. Our diversified nest egg, built in only a few hours per month, has ensured our financial future. Our first child has just been born and has an investment portfolio that all but guarantees she is already a 'time' millionaire.

So how did we do this and, more importantly, how can you?

I learned a lot in the wake of losing everything. I learned that I didn't want to go through the angst of having the financial carpet pulled out from under me again. I also learned that I didn't want my child to go through the same fear of debt and dead-end jobs that plagued me as I graduated from university into the jobless early 1990s recession and, which ultimately motivated my reckless speculation.

In the wake of catastrophic loss and debt I started my investment education all over again. I learned that only you can look out for your financial interests, and that most financial 'experts' have patchy knowledge at best and are more concerned with looking after their fees and bonuses than your money. I also learned that investing isn't as complicated as experts make it out to be and that making solid returns and building long term wealth is simply a matter of learning and applying a few core investing principles over time.

I've boiled these principles down into easy steps so you can build a powerful investment system that all but guarantees (there are no guarantees in investing) that your child will be set-up financially for life. This will alleviate a lifetime of stress and worry about money, and free your child to pursue a fulfilling life of interest and passion. Best of all, you can do this in mere hours per year and automate the system so it virtually runs itself, leaving you plenty of time to spend with your kids while they unknowingly become millionaires.

1

Everything You Need to Know About Investing

The Child Millionaire System – (Almost) as Easy as Buying Groceries

Investing can seem complicated to the uninitiated, but it doesn't have to be this way. The perception that you must read the financial press, know complex mathematics or have 'secret' insider knowledge is simply not true. Anyone can setup an investment portfolio for themselves or their child and grow rich. There's no secret to it once you understand the basics. As I'll show you in clear, easy-to-follow steps, investing really is (almost) as easy as opening a bank account and going shopping for groceries.

The system that follows is predominantly designed for creating a Child Millionaire and thus is geared towards very long time horizons. Unlike an actively managed investment portfolio with shorter time horizons where the risk and consequences of losing money are amplified, the Child Millionaire system is designed to be:

- Easy to set up and run with little or no knowledge of investment or economics, by absolutely anyone.
- Automated as much as possible and requiring little or no active management.
- A true robust investment system where you purchase and own real, wealth-generating assets, not a speculative bet or 'play' on the market. If you are looking to speculate or get rich quick then this system isn't for you. We are looking to build real, long-term wealth for your child.
- Not dependent on, or even concerned with, which way the market is headed.
- Geared to very long time horizons of 40–80 years where risk and volatility are flattened.

The principles of the system are also applicable to your own retirement planning if you have 20+ years to go. However, the system may not be suitable for shorter-term investment horizons such as saving for a house deposit. With shorter horizons, market volatility and risk are amplified, particularly *Black Swan* type events such as market crashes, which could lead to severe, if only temporary, losses of capital. As with all types of investment and any investment system, it is possible to lose money; however, I have a serious allergy to losing money so I've designed this system to minimize the chances of loss and maximize the potential for gain. Before you implement this system, please read the legal disclaimer at the front of this publication and proceed at your own risk.

The Goal

The goal is to setup a system to build a powerful Child Millionaire investment portfolio that requires little effort on your part, is mostly or entirely automated and which virtually guarantees your child will be an instant 'time millionaire' and at the same time to instil the benefits of investing, ownership and money smarts in your child.

The secret formula for the Child Millionaire system at its most basic is:

Regular investment (of the right kind) X re-investment (compounding) X time = Child Millionaire

It's (almost) that easy! But allow me to elaborate.

Ignore the Experts and Take Ownership and Control

The first step in creating a Child Millionaire is to ignore the advice of so-called financial experts, such as mutual fund sales people, and take ownership, control and responsibility for your own success. Financial experts project the image of knowing about the markets and where they are headed but they don't. In fact nobody knows what the market is going to do. If they did they wouldn't be selling mutual funds to unsuspecting parents, they'd be relaxing on a beach sipping mojitos with a very fat investment portfolio.

When you deal with financial industry 'experts' always ask yourself: 'where's the money?' If the person selling you something is driving an old beat-up car then they probably know very little. If they are driving a Mercedes then chances are they know a great deal about separating clients from their money through lucrative commissions and fees, but not necessarily how to manage your or anyone else's money.

Child Millionaire Secret Number 1: Ignore the So-called 'Experts'

I'm not saying you should dismiss wholesale what financial 'experts' are saying. However, whatever financial experts, advisors or alleged gurus say needs to be considered in the light of the reality that the financial services industry exists to serve itself and to make huge profits and bonuses funded out of your money in the form of fees, commissions and annual management charges. As such, the whole industry is underpinned by self-interest that is often at odds with your interests and as such it should be avoided except when absolutely necessary. In the pages that follow I'll show you a system that allows you to ignore the so-called experts, ignore what the markets are doing, minimize or even avoid all fees and generally send the experts packing.

Don't Save, Invest

So how do wealthy people achieve financial freedom and independence?

Certainly not by working hard and *saving*, which is what most working people try to do. No, what separates the financially rich from the financially poor is their attitude towards money. The financially rich see money as a resource to be used to make more money. It is this 'use-value' of money that's the lynchpin. Money to the financially rich is for acquiring ownership in high-quality businesses that pay the owner to own them. This is called *investing* and it's a world away from the 'saving' that most people pursue or the rampant casino-style speculation that characterizes so much of what passes for investing.

Creating a Child Millionaire starts by you changing your thinking. First you need to delete 'saving' from your vocabulary and thinking and replace it with 'investing'. You are no longer saving for your child's education or retirement, you are investing. Your child doesn't have a 'savings' account, they have an 'investment' account. What's the difference? A saver puts money in a bank where the interest of say 0.1%, or if you have a large enough deposit a 'high rate' of maybe 2.8%, is eroded by inflation that is two to ten times higher. This means that over time the saver actually loses money and is in effect paying the bank to store his or her money. Left long enough, your average bank account will eventually be reduced to virtually nothing by the ravages of inflation.

Conversely, an investor is someone who takes the money they save and puts it to use buying assets that provide a return or income stream. People who are financially rich are owners, poor people are savers. The difference is fundamental. You must become an owner!

Child Millionaire Secret Number 2: Become an Owner

Unlike the saver who puts money into the bank, an investor would purchase stock or 'shares' in the bank and thus becomes a part-owner of the bank. As an owner, the investor is entitled to part of the bank's profits, paid as dividends, which are the shareholder's share of the bank's profit. The profit is of course made by taking savers' money, which costs next to nothing, leveraging it many times over, and lending it out at higher rates of interest to mortgage holders, savers who dip into their overdraft or people with credit card debt. A bank share might 'yield' (pay an annual dividend) of 5%, which means that if you own $1,000 worth of shares you would receive $50 per annum compared with the $1–2 you'd earn from $1,000 in the same bank's regular savings account. If this dividend of $50 is reinvested into more shares then the next year you compound your return by earning 5% on $1,050 – i.e. your original $1,000 plus the dividend of $50 – so you'd earn $52.50 next year in dividends. This leads us to the third secret of creating a Child Millionaire.

The Magic of Compounding

Einstein called compounding or compound interest 'the greatest mathematical discovery of all time.'

Compounding simply means that any interest or dividend yield you receive on invested money in one year is added to the original investment the next year. In the second year you earn interest on the original investment *and* on the interest from the first year. In the third year you earn interest on the original investment plus interest on the interest made in the first and second years and so on. The annual gain starts small and looks insignificant but over time it starts to snowball.

Child Millionaire Secret Number 3: The Magic of Compounding or Compound Interest

Take the above example of a bank stock. Assume that every year we reinvest the dividend by purchasing more shares and we do the same year after year. Assume also that the share value grows by 3% a year and the dividend increases yearly at 8% (I'll explain all of this later). Here is what happens over 20 years through the power of compounding if you own the bank shares instead of having your money deposited in the bank.

Comparison of Owning Bank Shares Versus having a Deposit in the Bank

End of year	Bank deposit value, earning 0.1% per annum	Bank deposit value earning a 'high rate' of 2.8% per annum	Investment value by *owning* bank shares, 5% yield, dividend reinvested, annual share growth of 3%, dividend growth of 8%
1	$1,001.00	$1,028.00	$1,081.76
2	1,002.00	1,056.78	1,172.97
3	1,003.00	1,086.37	1,275.02
4	1,004.01	1,116.79	1,389.56
5	1,005.01	1,148.06	1,518.52
6	1,006.02	1,180.21	1,664.18
7	1,007.02	1,213.25	1,829.27
8	1,008.03	1,247.23	2,017.04
9	1,009.04	1,282.15	2,231.39
10	1,010.05	1,318.05	2,477.02
11	1,011.06	1,354.95	2,759.59
12	1,012.07	1,392.89	3,086.02
13	1,013.08	1,431.89	3,464.71
14	1,014.09	1,471.99	3,906.00
15	1,015.11	1,513.20	4,422.62
16	1,016.12	1,555.57	5,030.35
17	1,017.14	1,599.13	5,748.85
18	1,018.15	1,643.90	6,602.76
19	1,019.17	1,689.93	7,623.14
20	1,020.19	1,737.25	8,849.39

Pretty impressive. By owning shares in the bank instead of holding your money on deposit at 0.1%, you'd earn a staggering 389 times as much. Even at a 'high rate' of bank interest you'd still make 10.6 times as much by owning bank shares over a deposit. Is it any wonder that the rich are owners rather than savers?

But how powerful is the compound effect over large periods of time?

Manhattan for $24

Back in 1626, so the story goes, Peter Minuit bought the island of Manhattan in present-day New York from the local indigenous people for $24 and some trinkets. Most people would say that Peter Minuit made a shrewd investment and came out on top in the deal. However, had the sellers of Manhattan been able to invest their $24 at 8.92% per annum– the real long term 'compound annual growth rate' of the then-not-yet-created New York Stock Exchange (NYSE) *before* inflation – 385 years later in 2011, their investment portfolio would be worth a staggering $4,641,408,773,625,668.

That's $4.6 *trillion* dollars.

Even using the long term compound annual growth rate for the NYSE of 6.72% per annum *after* inflation, the $24 would have grown to $1,798,252,290,351 in today's dollars. That's $1.8 *trillion* dollars, or about one eighth the size of the entire gross domestic product (GDP) of the United States of $14.5 trillion.

Clearly the sellers had neither the knowledge nor the opportunity to invest their $24 but this example does illustrate next secret of creating a Child Millionaire and a vital part of compounding: time.

Child Millionaire Secret Number 4: Lots and lots of Time

The Rule of 72

Einstein discovered the 'Rule of 72,' which basically means that if you divide 72 by the interest rate you are receiving you will know how many years it will take to double your money. At 8% interest per annum it will take 9 years to double your money – i.e. 72 divided by 8 equals 9. The reverse also works. If you want to double your money in say 5 years then divide 72 by 5 and you will find out that you will need to earn 14.4% return on your money, compounded annually. What this illustrates is that either a high interest rate *or* a long period of time will result in rapid doubling and thus yield big results with compounding. When the two are combined the impact is dramatic.

As any investor knows, however, high rates of return are elusive and can't just be conjured up out of thin air. However, for the Child Millionaire portfolio, while we can't control the rate of return, we have the inherent advantage of lots and lots of time. Not enough time to squander it, but enough to turn almost any amount of money into a fortune.

The Power of Time and Compounding

Unlike middle-aged people investing for their retirement, with say 15 or 20 years to go, a newborn, who statistically is likely to live well into her 80s or beyond, has the advantage of 40, 50, 60 or more years on her side. This time side of the compounding formula can create truly staggering outcomes. Using the historic long-term rate of return on stocks, also known as 'equities,' of 8.92% compound annual growth rate before inflation, here is what would happen to $1,000 invested when a baby is born.

Future value of $1,000 earning 8.92% compounded annually

End of year	Value
1	$1,089
20	$5,523
40	$30,500
60	$168,445
80	$930,273
100	$5,137,635

The Economy is Unpredictable

With long time frames for compounding in the Child Millionaire portfolio, we have the advantage of not needing to worry about what is happening to the economy or financial markets in the short or medium term. This is a good thing because nobody knows what is going to happen to interest rates, unemployment rates, GDP or any other lead indicators. Anyone who claims he does is either deluded or lying.

As a case in point of how unpredictable the future is and how often the 'experts' get it wrong, have a look at the following graph from the Federal Reserve Bank of Philadelphia. The blue line is the real inflation-adjusted annual change in GDP for the US over the past 40 years. You can see how it has moved all over the place during boom and busts in the economic cycle. The red line shows the consensus view of economists on where US GDP was headed. You can see how the economists missed all of the booms and busts even when we were right in the middle of one such as the 2008 meltdown.

Source: Federal Reserve Bank of Philadelphia   Actual data through Jun 2010; projection through Sep 2011

The economists can't get it right and we aren't likely to either because there is simply too much (or sometimes too little) data and too many ways to interpret how different economic and non-economic forces interact. So in response to this uncertain backdrop, we need a category of assets to invest in and a system that can be set up and (almost) forgotten about, generating high returns and letting you get on with football practice or fishing or whatever other activity brings you and your child joy, knowing he or she is already financially secure regardless of what happens in the economy or markets.

So against an uncertain and unpredictable backdrop, where do we put our Child Millionaire investment money to ensure maximum compound growth?

2

The Power of Dividends – Getting Paid to be an Owner

Where Do We Invest?

There are a variety of types of investment available to the average 'retail' investor. These include government bonds, corporate bonds issued by companies, mortgage-backed securities, precious metals, growth stocks or dividend paying shares issued by companies and traded on the various stock exchanges.

All of these asset classes perform differently under various macro-economic conditions. However they all require, with the exception of one, a mixture of careful watching of various economic indicators and the ability to interpret what is going to happen next in the large-scale economic picture. Yet, as we know, the future is unpredictable.

Bonds, for example, are vulnerable to government interest rate changes, and although they can perform well under certain conditions they require you to keep an eye on the direction of interest rates and other headline economic data. Likewise, precious metals perform well in certain conditions, particularly in low-interest-rate environments and in the exceptional cases of currency debasement through 'quantitative easing,' but they are highly volatile and speculative. Mortgage-backed instruments are constrained by interest rates and lack the ability for rapid growth. As the ongoing housing meltdown in the US makes clear, they are also not nearly as secure as their sales proponents would suggest.

None of this will do for the hands-off Child Millionaire portfolio. So what *will* work then?

Shares that Pay Dividends

As we now know, an investor is an owner of a company and so we want the Child Millionaire portfolio to be a vehicle for company ownership. So where does a would-be owner with only $1,000 go to buy into a high-quality business cheaply and without needing to know which way the economy is headed? Going back to the story of our 1980 Johnson & Johnson portfolio in the Introduction, the answer is the stock market. The only asset class that gives us what we want for the Child Millionaire portfolio – ownership, high compound growth and hands-off management, all without needing or caring to know where the economy is headed – is shares in companies. But not just any old share in any old company. As I'll explain later in detail, our Child Millionaire portfolio is going to be composed entirely of one type of investment: *high-quality dividend-paying shares in companies that increase their dividends year after year.* Such companies, as I'll explain, are sometimes called 'dividend aristocrats.' But before we get to this let's talk a bit about stock markets and investing in shares.

What is a Stock or Share Market?

A stock or share market or exchange is simply a place to buy and sell the shares of companies listed on the exchange so that companies can raise money.

There are many stock markets and they are measured by indices that track the performance of a selection of companies within the market. The New York Stock Exchange (NYSE) is measured by the Dow Jones Industrial Average (DJIA), AKA 'The Dow,' which is comprised of the top 30 companies on the NYSE. The Standard and Poor 500 (S&P 500) index tracks a broader selection of 500 top US-based companies across various US stock markets including the tech-focused NASDAQ exchange. In Canada there is the resource-heavy Toronto Stock Exchange (TSX) tracked by the S&P/TSX Composite Index of companies comprising about 70% of the market's value. In the UK, the finance- and mining-heavy London Stock Exchange is tracked by the FTSE 100 index, comprised of the 100 largest companies on the exchange. There are also innumerable other stock markets and indices such as the German DAX, the Japanese Nikkei and markets in Singapore, Australia and other countries.

Ultimately a stock market is simply a meeting place between buyers and sellers for segments of companies represented by small units called 'stocks' or 'shares' (the terms are interchangeable). By dividing a company up into millions of tiny shares the barrier to owning part of the company is lowered and the shares become highly liquid, meaning they are easily bought and sold on a stock exchange, making it relatively easy for a company to raise money for expansion. In fact the shares of some very large companies on the world's stock markets are bought and sold by the millions every day by investment funds, pension funds and individuals, with thousands of shares changing hands every second.

What you need to be absolutely clear about is that the stock market itself is not an investment. The stock market is simply a market or mechanism that allows us to purchase shares in high-quality companies in the same way that you might purchase high-quality fruit at a fruit market. Accessing this vast marketplace via online brokerage or trading accounts charging as little as \$10-30 per transaction allows virtually anyone to buy part of a high-quality company at a very low price. Never in history has it been easier or cheaper to become part-owner of the top companies in the world. And with ownership comes privilege.

What are 'Shares' or 'Stocks'?

Shares are basically certificates – these days usually in electronic form but still available as paper certificates – which provide proof of your share of ownership of whatever company issued them. As a 'shareholder' you are entitled to part of the company's profits or losses. Companies issue shares in order to raise capital for organic or internally driven growth, or for expansion through the acquisition of other companies.

Growth Stocks versus Dividend-Paying Stocks

When a company earns a profit, the board of directors can choose to retain the profit within the company and use it to fund expansion of the business or distribute some or all of the profit as a dividend.

If the profit is retained within that company, over time this means that the company will in theory grow in size and market share, and potentially in future profitability, and thus in value on the stock market. This is the common model for smaller companies or 'small caps,' which are focused on *growth.*

On the flip side, unlike smaller 'growth-oriented' companies, larger, more mature companies tend to pay out part of their profits as a dividend to shareholders and retain a portion internally to fund expansion. Of the many thousands of companies listed on the various stock exchanges, it is typically the largest companies, usually the dominant ones in their sector, be it oil, banking, healthcare, telecommunications or consumer products that pay part of their profits to shareholders in the form of dividends.

The size of some of these 'large-cap' or 'blue chip' companies makes rapid growth difficult, if not impossible. A $177 billion company like Johnson & Johnson simply can't grow at 25–30% per year like a smaller company because of limits on the size of the market and the resources required. Consequently, large, stable, dominant companies tend to grow at more modest rates, though some still grow at 10–15% per year or more. Although slower-growing, because of their market dominance every additional product or sale large companies make year-on-year tends to add to the bottom-line profit because they already have the manufacturing, sales, marketing and distribution infrastructure in place. Thus large companies are often more profitable than smaller ones, but they grow at a slower rate.

But How Do I Make Money from Shares?

Coming back to how you make money in stocks, there are basically two ways.

Capital Gains

If you buy a share and over time its value increases because the company grows in size and profitability, or is purchased at a premium by a larger company and then you sell for a higher price than you paid, then the difference is a 'capital gain.' This is called a 'capital gain' because you have literally had a gain in the size of your money or 'capital.'

For example, if you purchase 100 shares of XYZ Company at $10 per share your total capital investment is 100 X $10 = $1,000. If in five years the share has gone up to $20 and you sell it, you will receive $2,000 (excluding fees), i.e. $20 X 100 shares = $2,000. Subtracting your initial capital investment of $1,000 from the $2,000 means you have realized a capital gain of $1,000. In other words you have made a 100% return over five years.

Correspondingly, you can make capital losses. If XYZ Company is poorly managed or overtaken by competitors, its value could drop. Say after five years it is only worth $5 per share and you decide to sell. You receive $5 X 100 shares = $500, which means you have lost 50% of your original $1,000.

In the case above, money you have in shares of XYZ Company is not generating any sort of cash dividend. You are instead relying on hope and the prospect of growth in the company, and thus capital growth or appreciation, to supply you with your return over time. This return is only realized when you sell the stock. As I mentioned, most companies listed on stock exchanges are small or mid-cap companies that don't pay a dividend and are focused on growth. Sometimes the growth is spectacular and in the hundreds or even thousands of percentage points per year. This is especially the case in technology or mining sectors if a company creates a revolutionary product or strikes a huge mineral deposit. However, more often the reverse happens and a company has a catastrophic failure, loses much of its value or goes bankrupt, and shareholders lose their money.

Dividends

With larger mid- and large-cap companies, the growth rate is substantially reduced and so is the potential for capital appreciation of the company and shares though this can and still does happen, just at much more modest rates. However, the compensation for this lower growth rate is that these companies often pay cash dividends to shareholders. In addition, as dominant players in their industries, such companies tend to be very large and thus well insulated from bankruptcy, and they are often able to operate across international boundaries, thus reducing the political or economic risk of operating only in one country or region. This size and reach allows such companies to participate in booming markets such as in parts of East Asia, India and Latin America, thus offsetting the poor economic conditions in Europe and North America, even if these companies are based in London, New York or Toronto.

How Dividends Work

As mentioned above, dividends represent a portion of a company's profits. For example, let's assume that ABC Company has issued a total of 100 million shares, which are owned by thousands of individual 'retail' investors, pension funds and mutual and other funds as well as company directors. If the shares are currently trading on a stock market for $50 per share then the company has a market capitalization or 'market cap' of $5 billion (100 million shares X $50 per share = $5 billion), making it a large mid-cap company. If the company earns a net profit of $500 million then this equals $5 per share ($500 million ÷ 100 million shares = $5 per share). If the company has a 'pay-out rate' of 50% then $2.50 of the $5 profit is issued as a dividend to shareholders for each share they own, while the remaining $2.50 is retained internally to fund company growth.

The $2.50 divided by the share price of $50 = 5%. This means that ABC Company's shares 'yield' 5%. If you own 20 shares of the company your cost to purchase the shares is $1,000, and with a 5% yield you earn $50 per year as a dividend for owning part of the company. Because the company pay-out ratio is only 50%, it has retained the other 50% of its net profits of $250 million ($2.50 per share) to use for research and development, market expansion, acquisitions or other activities that result in growth. Over time – barring some sort of catastrophe – this should mean that the value of the company increases, and thus its share price will also appreciate. Then if you sell your shares at a future date you will (probably) make a capital gain, and in the intervening time you will have been banking dividends paid in cash.

So What Does this Mean for the Child Millionaire System?

The Child Millionaire portfolio is going to be comprised *entirely* of shares in high-quality *dividend-paying* companies, because these companies provide the best of all possible worlds. They are usually serious, even dominant players in their sectors; they often have global reach and can tap into fast-growing markets; and unlike small, riskier companies, *they are paying you to own them* in the form of dividends.

Historically, research shows that dividends matter more than almost anything else in stock market returns over time and dividend-paying shares dramatically outperform growth shares over time. They matter so much that the entire Child Millionaire portfolio system is built on them. In fact, *without dividends it would be difficult, if not impossible, to create a Child Millionaire.* As an investor you should never, *ever*, buy a share if it doesn't pay a dividend, otherwise you are simply gambling.

The Power of Dividend Growth

Yet dividends themselves are only part of the story. As attractive as a 5% yield on a share might be, especially compared to 0.1% on your money in a bank account, this isn't going to do the full job of making a millionaire out of your child unless you start with a large amount of money. We need to turbo-charge the Child Millionaire portfolio through *dividend growth*.

The power of dividend growth is rooted in the compound effect. Recall that the impact of compounding starts small and when time is added it has a tremendous impact. Even at a yield of 5% our money can multiply dramatically over time. Consider the shares in ABC Company. Starting with 20 shares X $50 per share = $1,000, with the shares yielding 5% as a dividend, the table below shows how your Child Millionaire portfolio would play out over the next 60 years if you reinvest the dividend and the shares grow in value at 3% per annum but there is *no dividend growth over time*.

End of year	Value, 5% yield and 3% share appreciation per annum, **no dividend growth**
1	$1,082
20	$3,832
40	$10,507
60	$23,917

Not bad, but not great.

Now let's see what happens if we have consistent *dividend growth* over time.

Let's assume that ABC Company is a real dynamo in their sector (like Johnson & Johnson) and they are able to increase their profits year-on-year and thus they increase their dividend every year as well. So in the first year the company pays out $2.50 per share, or a 5% yield on a $50 share. Next year the company increases its profits by selling more products and expanding into new markets, say China or India or Brazil, or by raising prices for its products, which are in high demand. The next year the company makes a profit of $540 million, or $5.40 per share, and pays out 50% of this or $2.70 to each shareholder. This $2.70 is 8% more than the $2.50 you were paid the year before so you are now earning $2.70 on each share and the dividend is increasing at 8% per annum.

Now, let's say that the next year the company does the same thing. The profits increase again and the dividend also increases again by 8%, so the $2.70 dividend goes up by 8%, meaning that the next year the dividend is $2.92 per share (108% X $2.70 = $2.92). You are now in year three, earning $2.92 on your original investment of $50 per share, so the yield on your money has increased to 5.84% ($2.92 ÷ $50 X 100% = 5.84%). What's going on here is that your dividends are experiencing the compounding effect. If this carries on year after year then the power of compounding causes the dividends to balloon over time.

Yet, impressive as this sounds, there is even more that can be done. If you take the dividend every year and reinvest it into more shares then your original 20 shares will grow in number every year by the value of the dividend. So let's say that at the end of year one you have 20 shares that cost $50 each and you are paid a dividend of 5% or $2.50 per share X 20 shares = $50. If this $50 is then used to purchase another share, at the beginning of year two you will now have 21 shares, which at the end of year two are yielding $2.70 per share. At this point you are banking $56.70 in dividends ($2.70 X 21 shares = $56.70), so your dividend payments have now increased by a massive 13.4% over the first year. If you then take this $56.70 and purchase more shares the compounding effect continues.

You are now benefiting from a compounding of your original investment of $1,000 through the repurchase of more shares *and* you are benefiting from the compounding of the share dividend itself. The impact is staggering. Here is how it plays out over 60 years for your $1,000, assuming ongoing reinvestment of the dividend into more shares and constant dividend growth of 8% per year, shares yielding 5% and annual share appreciation of 3%, compared to the same shares without dividend growth.

Comparison of growth of $1,000 with no dividend growth versus 8% per annum dividend growth

End of year	Portfolio value, dividend yield of 5% reinvested and 3% share appreciation per annum, **no dividend growth**	Portfolio value, dividend yield of 5% reinvested and 3% share appreciation per annum **plus dividend growth of 8% per annum**
1	$1,082	$1,082
20	$3,832	$8,849
40	$10,507	$902,976
60	$23,917	$35,893,197,894

Yes, that final figure is $35.9 *billion* dollars. This is the staggering power of compound growth when turbo charged with *compound dividend growth.*

Child Millionaire Secret Number 5: Only Buy Shares that Pay a Dividend and that Have Annual Dividend Growth

By purchasing shares in companies that pay dividends, increase their dividends over time and retain some money internally for growth, your Child Millionaire portfolio gains in three powerful ways: through the cash dividend payment, through the impact of the rising dividend and through share value appreciation. This is a triple win you can *only* get from dividend-paying shares – no other asset class offers this level of return – and, best of all, it comes with the security of regular, growing, low-taxed cash dividend payments.

Companies that have a long track record of paying dividends and increasing the dividends year after year are often referred to as 'dividend aristocrats'. It is these companies that we want to own in the Child Millionaire portfolio, and I'll get to how we find these sorts of companies shortly, but for now let's talk a bit about 'volatility.'

3

Market Volatility

Why Stock Market Crashes Are Good for the Child Millionaire

In the last chapter I mentioned that the third way you win with dividend-paying companies is by the share price increasing over time to reflect the growth of the company fuelled by retained earnings.

It would be nice if share prices always went up without interruption. However, this is rarely, if ever, the case even if a company reports uninterrupted and ever-growing profits. Shares trade on the open market and for every buyer there is a seller, and vice versa. One person or fund manager's reason for selling or buying may have little to do with the value or quality of the company in question and lots to do with personal, policy or macro-economic issues. Or it might have to do with market sentiment and momentum, which can drag the shares in all companies in one sector or market in one direction or another irrespective of an individual company's financial performance. This up and down movement in individual share prices or in whole markets is often referred to as 'volatility.' The years 2008 and 2009 displayed tremendous, perhaps even record, volatility across all shares and markets as the global financial crisis unfolded, and stocks plunged and soared almost at random and without warning.

So while, generally speaking, high-quality companies and their shares will tend to appreciate or gain value over the long term, over shorter time horizons volatility can move the price all over the place. There can be great waves of panic leading people to sell when a market is plunging for fear that it will never stop dropping, such as in March of 2009. Or there can be great exuberance, with people buying at the top of the market, such as the summer of 2007, when greed takes over, the market seems to have no upward limit and those who don't 'get in' fear that they will lose out.

All of this volatility favours traders and speculators over investors, and paying too much attention to it isn't healthy for you or your Child Millionaire portfolio. Believe me that until you experience the gut-wrenching turmoil of a plunging market with all of your net worth riding on a few speculative stocks, as I did in 2000, you don't truly understand the fear that traders and speculators talk about. It's easy to think you can be stoical during a market plunge, but the reality is that very, very few can, and even these brave or stupid souls spend sleepless nights questioning their assumptions and their sanity.

Because the Child Millionaire portfolio consists of high-quality, large-cap, dividend-paying stocks, the volatility is automatically reduced as these sorts of large stable companies, though affected by large-scale market movements such as those in 2008 and 2009, are affected to a much lesser degree than medium or small-cap shares. Also, because these companies pay a dividend, the share prices tend not to plunge as far because there is a floor to values set by how much dividend income the shares provide. So automatically we have some stability with these sorts of companies.

Yet how do we deal with or even benefit from market volatility, even market crashes, in the Child Millionaire investment portfolio? The answer is that we ignore it and let the market take care of itself and use the highs and lows to our automatic advantage through a concept known as 'dollar (or pound) cost averaging.'

Dollar/Pound Cost Averaging

Dollar or pound cost averaging is a method of reducing your risk and using volatility to get an overall lower average price for shares by buying more shares when the shares are cheap and buying fewer when the shares are expensive. It's an easy concept to understand in practice and it can add tremendously to your Child Millionaire portfolio. Best of all, it's basically automatic.

To see how dollar cost averaging works, let's go back to our example of ABC Company. For the sake of clarity, in the following example I'll use reasonably large numbers; however, the effect is the same regardless of the amount of money. Let's assume that our initial investment is 100 shares at $50 each for a total of $5,000. Let's assume, as is typical with dividend-paying companies, that ABC Company pays its dividends quarterly, so in the first year the $2.50 dividend per share is paid $0.625 on 31 March, $0.625 on 30 June, $0.625 on 30 September and the final $0.625 on 31

December. Assume that when we receive the quarterly dividends into our Child Millionaire portfolio, we reinvest the money by purchasing more shares in the same company. This is called 'dividend reinvestment' and, as discussed above, it's a form of compounding because the new shares we purchase will also earn future dividend income, which will also be reinvested thereby continuing the cycle.

Now let's assume that the general market is highly volatile, as it has been in recent years, and while ABC Company is solid, profitable and stable, the share price is moving all over the place from the $50 price at which we bought our initial 100 shares for $5,000. Keep in mind that this volatility doesn't affect the dividend amount – i.e. the $2.50 per share – but as you will see it does impact the yield.

Now assume that when the first dividend is paid on 31 March, the share price has plunged to $40. Our dividend payment is 100 shares X $0.625 = $62.50 and we immediately use this money to purchase more shares. At $40 a share we are able to purchase 1.56 shares (I'll explain later how partial shares can be purchased at low or no cost, so bear with me for now). These additional 1.56 shares will be added to our 100 shares and will pay a dividend within this year, but for simplicity let's assume that any shares we purchase in each quarter don't pay a dividend until the following year.

On 30 June we again receive our dividend payment of $62.50, but now the share price on the market is $30, so our $62.50 buys 2.08 shares. On 30 September we again receive $62.50, but now the share price has soared to $60, so we are only able to purchase 1.04 shares; and then on 31 December when we receive our final $62.50, the share price is back where it started at $50 so we are able to purchase 1.25 shares.

Here is how the share purchases look:

Date	Dividend earned on 100 shares	Share price	Shares purchased	Cumulative shares
31 March	$62.50	$40	1.56	1.56
30 June	$62.50	$30	2.08	3.64
30 Sep	$62.50	$60	1.04	4.68
31 Dec	$62.50	$50	1.25	5.93

Average share price: $250 in total dividends ÷ 5.93 shares = $42.16 per share.

As you can see, over the course of the year the share price fluctuated wildly, perhaps because of a second global financial crisis, or high unemployment, or food riots in India, or a hurricane, or any number of other reasons; however, our dividend didn't change because it is based on company profitability, not the share price.

Over the course of the year we were able to purchase an additional 5.93 shares with our annual dividends of $250 for an average share price of $42.16 per share ($250 ÷ 5.93 shares = $42.16). Yet at the beginning and end of the year the price was $50 and only twice during our purchases was it near to $40. Because we purchased shares every quarter we achieved an *average price* that is very favourable and we smoothed out the spikes and troughs of volatility by automatically purchasing fewer shares when the price was high at $60 and more shares when the price was low at $30. This means that over the course of the year we ended up with an average price on the new shares below our original $50.

The following year we now get a dividend of $2.50 per year on these new shares, which cost an average of $42.16 each, and so the yield has now increased from 5% to $2.50 ÷ $42.16 = 5.93% on the new 'dollar cost-averaged' shares. If the dividend increases by 8% the following year to $2.70, then the yield on these new shares will be $2.70 ÷ $42.16 = 6.40%, so the yield on the shares we own is starting to increase over time.

I know what you are thinking – why not buy all the shares when the price is $30 and none when it is $60? This strategy is known as 'market timing.' Sure, if we had a crystal ball we would only purchase at the lowest point and avoid the peak, but the reality is that the gyrations of the market are unpredictable no matter what your financial advisor or mutual fund salesman says. If you doubt this, ask 'where's the money?' and remember that if anyone could predict that market he or she would be on a beach sipping cocktails. Market timing sounds easy with hindsight, but it isn't when you're looking forward. Even those who are halfway good at it, and there aren't many, spend endless hours pouring over technical charts, running computer simulations and trying to control their emotions of fear and greed. Don't you have something better to do than become a 'technical analyst,' like going swimming with your kids or having a nap? Remember, all evidence suggests that market timing is for fools, gamblers or the very few who are brilliant or, more likely, very, very lucky.

Child Millionaire Secret Number 6: Dollar/Pound Cost Averaging

The best thing about dollar cost averaging, besides giving you a better overall price for the shares in your Child Millionaire portfolio, is that it removes *emotion* from the investment equation by making volatility irrelevant. Or perhaps, to be more precise, it uses volatility to your advantage. In fact the less attention you pay to the share price and the financial news the better. Simply let the automatic reinvestment take care of the volatility problem while you get on with football practice or picnicking or fishing. Meanwhile your friends, who may be 'playing the market' (speculating while thinking they are investing) and holding non-dividend-paying growth stocks – perhaps even ultra-speculative 'penny' shares – sweat, lie awake at night and devour the financial press trying to read something into every piece of financial news. Inevitably they will end up buying in at the top, when they come late to the party and greed (or the fear of not making money) takes over, and sell out at the bottom in a panicked frenzy. While they agonize and watch their portfolios crumble and have visions of their children flipping burgers for life, you relax, get paid to own your companies and continue to accumulate shares. When the stock market crashes you (discreetly) rub your hands together knowing you are purchasing more high-quality stocks at a lower price. By using dollar cost averaging, volatility becomes the friend rather than the enemy of the Child Millionaire.

The Power of Regular Contributions

Yet dollar cost averaging can be made to work *even harder* for you. In addition to dividend reinvestment, it is very easy to contribute to your Child Millionaire investment account automatically on a monthly, quarterly or annual basis and use this money to purchase more shares on the same regular cycle.

For example, say you can invest $100 a month into your Child Millionaire portfolio. You may even prefer to do this from the start if you can't afford an initial lump sum. You set up this contribution to come out of your bank account and be deposited into your Child Millionaire portfolio as you might with any other regular savings or bill payment. Let's assume that every quarter, as the dividend payment arrives in the Child Millionaire portfolio account and is used to purchase additional shares, the $300 that will have accumulated from your regular savings is also used to purchase more shares. So in our example above, on 31 March and each subsequent quarter, you have $62.50 from dividends and $300 from regular contributions, giving you $362.50 to invest.

This is how your quarterly share purchases would look.

Date	Dividend on 100 shares	Quarterly savings at $100/mth	Share price	Shares purchased	Cumulative shares
31 Mar	$62.50	$300	$40	9.06	9.06
30 June	$62.50	$300	$30	12.08	21.14
30 Sept	$62.50	$300	$60	6.04	27.18
31 Dec	$62.50	$300	$50	7.25	34.43

Average share price: $250 in total dividends + $1,200 in regular contributions = $1,450 ÷ 34.43 shares = $42.16 per share.

By the beginning of the next year you now have 134.43 shares that, assuming the dividend increases by 8% to $2.70, are going to earn you $362.96 in dividends ($90.74 quarterly), which you then reinvest. Now remember that the company is only paying out half of its profits as dividends, while retaining the other half to fuel continued growth and development. This growth is evidenced by growing profits, and thus dividends, and it ultimately drives the share price upwards. Let's assume that over time, after accounting for the 'noise' of volatility, the value of the company increases at a conservative rate of 3% per year, which is around the rate of inflation in many developed countries. Over time this will be reflected in the average share price irrespective of how volatility moves the price around on a daily, weekly or monthly basis. If you and then your child continue the $100 per month payment into the Child Millionaire portfolio let's see what impact this has.

Assumptions: start with 100 shares of ABC Company for initial price of $50 each, so an initial investment of $5,000, currently paying $2.50 (5% yield), with the dividend increasing at 8% per annum, and regular monthly contributions of $100 for the duration. Assuming that volatility averages out over time to an even curve otherwise my calculations would be enormously complicated and the share price increases by 3% per annum, here is how the portfolio would look over 60 years.

End of year	Portfolio value	Cumulative number of shares	Annual dividend income
1	$6,548	127	$277
20	$139,790	1,548	$15,437
40	$14,919,814	91,475	$3,825,766
60	$993,185,703,925	2,013,664,520	$309,678,000,000

Almost unbelievable but true – the numbers don't lie. Your child would be a millionaire at age 31 and able to draw a hefty and low-taxed income from dividends if he or she chose to, and a very, very wealthy person by retirement.

If you think the assumptions for ABC Company are a wee bit optimistic, consider that for the 30 years from 1980–2010, Johnson & Johnson's average annual compound growth was 12.99%, the yield has generally been in the region of 2.8% and annual dividend growth has been a staggering 13.57%.

Ok, but what if you don't have an initial investment?

Well, then start with $100 and contribute on a monthly basis. With no initial investment and by contributing $100 a month for the duration – you for 18 years and your child after that – here is how the portfolio would look with ABC Company.

End of year	Portfolio value	Cumulative number of shares	Annual dividend income
1	$1,139	22	$23
20	$95,543	1,058	$10,528
40	$10,404,932	63,794	$2,667,999
60	$413,719,714,455	1,404,438,281	$215,986,000,000

So even with only a $100 regular monthly contribution your child would become a millionaire when he or she turned 32 and by age 60 would have a truly massive portfolio, all without an initial lump sum investment.

Ok, all this sounds good. Perhaps a little too good. Because what about inflation and risk?

4

Inflation and Risk

Why Doing Nothing is More Dangerous than Doing Something

Inflation and the Future Value of Money

We live in interesting times. Loose monetary policy in the form of historically low interest rates and quantitative easing by central banks to shore up the global financial system, coupled with simultaneous demand for resources and higher wages in Asia, is stoking inflation. We know inflation is coming, but we don't know when or how much we will face in the future because it is historically unpredictable.

So how do we ensure that our Child Millionaire portfolio doesn't end up being eroded by inflation? Well, it's difficult. Research shows that pretty much all asset classes except perhaps commodities such as oil, gas, metals and minerals are hurt by inflation. However, predicting inflation in the short term, let alone over the timeframe of a Child Millionaire portfolio, is impossible.

In low or moderately low inflationary environments, such as the past 15 years, the value of a Child Millionaire portfolio should keep pace or even exceed inflation because large companies with 'must-have' products tend to be able to increase their prices, and thus profits, as their costs increase. The value of companies on stock markets can also appreciate as inflation rises, largely shielding the portfolio from inflation's potentially corrosive effects. From 1926 through 2008, the total US stock market, as measured by the University of Chicago CRSP 1-10 Index, outpaced inflation by an average of 6.16% per year.

However, in very highly inflationary environments such as the period 1973–81, there isn't much protection in any asset class except perhaps commodities, precious metals and possibly bonds at the right time in the economic cycle. However, during the very high inflation of the 1970s, some large, well-managed companies with high returns on equity were able to provide a good inflation hedge. Because the Child Millionaire portfolio has the massive advantage of time on its side, large dividend-paying companies, especially those exposed to the high-growth markets of Asia, are a pretty decent inflation hedge. So unless you are experienced with asset classes such as gold and commodities, I'd suggest you stick with the large dividend paying companies and a regular investment plan, and don't get too worked up about hedging for inflation.

In the big picture, though, how might inflation impact the future value of the Child Millionaire portfolio if we stick with dividend-paying shares through thick and thin? Let's assume a long-term average inflation rate of 3.82%. This includes times of very low inflation and spikes of high inflation, but is the average in the US over the time period from January 1914 when the US government first started tracking inflation until December 2010. Going forward, this number could be reasonably accurate or wildly inaccurate, we just don't know. In the UK over the past 80 years the numbers are reasonably similar.

At 3.82% the long-term inflation rate is corrosive to investments and the impact it will have on your child's future purchasing power is significant. Over 20, 40, 60 and 80 years here is what happens to the purchasing power of one dollar or pound.

The impact of 3.82% inflation on the purchasing power of $1 in today's money

Number of years	Future amount needed to equal the purchasing power of $1 today	Future value of $1
20	$2.12	$0.47
40	$4.48	$0.22
60	$9.48	$0.11
80	$20.07	$0.05

What this means is that if inflation averages 3.82% long-term then to buy a doughnut that costs you $1 today will require $2.12 in 20 years, $4.48 in 40 years, $9.48 in 60 years and in 80 years that same doughnut will cost you $20.07. You've probably noticed this inflationary effect on the price of chocolate bars or cinema tickets from when you were a kid until the present. Flipped around, the reverse of this is true – so $1 will only be worth $0.47

in twenty years – and in 80 years it will have lost a whopping 95% of its value and only be worth $0.05.

The impact of inflation on the Child Millionaire portfolio is potentially quite substantial though certainly not catastrophic, because of the power of compound return and time. Let's see how the model Child Millionaire portfolio would play out without, and then with, long-term average inflation of 3.82%, and how this will impact our child's purchasing power.

Assumptions: start with 100 shares of ABC Company for initial price of $50 each, so an initial investment of $5,000 currently paying a 5% yield, with the dividend increasing at 8% per annum, and regular contributions of $100 for the duration, not increased by the rate of inflation, and share price appreciation of 3% per annum. Because we aren't increasing the $100 monthly contribution, in 20 years it will only be equal to $47, and in 80 years only equal to $5 per month. Absolute or 'nominal' value of portfolio and dividend income i.e. what your portfolio account statement would actually show is as follows.

'Nominal' portfolio value *without* accounting for inflation

Years	Portfolio value in absolute or 'nominal' terms	Portfolio annual dividend income in absolute or 'nominal' terms
20	$139,790	$15,437
40	$14,919,814	$3,825,766
60	$593,185,703,925	$309,678,000,000

Next is what the portfolio value and dividend income would look like after being ravaged by 3.82% annual inflation, expressed in the purchasing power of today's dollars i.e. these are what the above values would equate to today.

Portfolio value *after* 3.82% annual inflation

Years	Portfolio value in purchasing power equivalent to today	Portfolio annual dividend income in purchasing power equivalent to today
20	$65,939	$7,282
40	$3,330,316	$853,966
60	$62,572,331,637	$32,666,455,696

So after 40 years your Child Millionaire portfolio would have an absolute or 'nominal' value of $14,919,814; your child would be well into the millionaire category and earning $3,825,766 in annual dividend income from the portfolio. By age 60, the numbers simply become ridiculously large. However, after taking the corrosive effects of inflation into account, after 40 years the $14,919,814 nominal value of the portfolio would only be worth the equivalent of $3,330,316 in today's dollars and generate an income equal to $853,966 in today's dollars. You can see how much less this is than the absolute or nominal numbers; however, it is still a considerable sum of money for a 40th birthday present. So although inflation continues to ravage the portfolio, because of the power of compounding and time, the compounding return on shares with rising dividends and appreciation should still outstrip the compounding impact of inflation.

To achieve these figures, no tax has been deducted and money can't be withdrawn along the way, or the compounding will be diminished. The example also assumes that you and then your child contribute a non-inflation-adjusted $100 per month for the duration. In all probability, though, your child will be earning employment or business income in the future, and with good investing habits it seems reasonable that he or she could contribute substantially more to the portfolio over time. So the monthly contribution might start at $100 and as earnings grow your child might work up to investing ten ($1,000 per month) or even 100 ($10,000 per month) times as much per month, truly sending an already substantial Child Millionaire portfolio into the financial stratosphere.

What about Persistent High Inflation?

But what if inflation is much higher in the future than in the past? A growing global population is increasing the demand for scarce resources such as oil, gas, water and agricultural goods. Coupled with rising incomes in Asia, especially in 'the world's workshop' of China, there is upwards pressure on the price of manufactured goods as well. These macro-level changes suggest that future inflation could be much higher than in the past. What might average inflation of 5%, 7.5% or even 10% do to the purchasing power of today's money, and thus a Child Millionaire portfolio?

The impact of high inflation rates on purchasing power of $1 in today's money

Number of years	Future amount needed to equal the purchasing power of $1 today			
	3.82% inflation	5% inflation	7.5% inflation	10% inflation
20	$2.12	$2.65	$4.25	$6.73
40	$4.48	$7.04	$18.04	$45.30
60	$9.48	$18.68	$76.65	$304.48
80	$20.07	$49.56	$325.59	$2,048.40

Number of years	Future value of $1			
	3.82% inflation	5% inflation	7.5% inflation	10% inflation
20	$0.47	$0.38	$0.24	$0.15
40	$0.22	$0.14	$0.06	$0.02
60	$0.11	$0.05	$0.013	$0.003
80	$0.05	$0.02	$0.003	$0.00049

So to take the worst case scenario above, in 80 years at 10% average annual inflation, a $1 doughnut would cost $2048.40. In other words, $1 in today's money would be reduced in value to $0.00049. Here is how persistent inflation of 10% would affect the model portfolio above.

Portfolio value after 10% annual inflation

Years	Portfolio value in purchasing power equivalent to today	Portfolio annual dividend income in purchasing power equivalent to today
20	$20,474	$2,294
40	$329,356	$84,454
60	$1,948,192,669	$1,017,071,729

So clearly inflation is powerful and corrosive, and we *must* take it into account. Severe inflation will have an equally severe impact. However the high-quality dividend-paying share-based Child Millionaire portfolio would still continue to outpace inflation.

What the divergent results above illustrate is that pinpointing both future inflation and future returns isn't really possible, and the best we can aim for is a *range* of good probable outcomes. What we do know for certain is that if we fail to invest anything then our future returns will be zero and there is a substantial probability that our child would face a very challenging financial future in a hyper-competitive world. What we also know is that *any* investment above zero will give the child a financial head start. Exactly how much of a head start depends on how much we invest, our assumptions and, ultimately, how reality plays out. Different inputs and assumptions will result in vastly different outcomes. However, rather than doing nothing in the face of uncertainty and simply hoping for the best, which is a strategy that can only result in failure, we can at least aim for a target and then do as much as possible to achieve success within a range of possible assumptions about inflation and future returns.

If you'd like to run your own inflation calculations at different rates of inflation over different periods of time, click here for a handy inflation calculator.

This discussion of inflation is in many respects about the issue of risk, to which we now turn.

Risk

You've probably heard that risk and returns go hand-in-hand. But what are the risks to the Child Millionaire portfolio?

Risk, in investment terms, is basically the probability, or possibility, that you will lose your capital if something negative happens to the company or companies you own because of the sector they are in, the overall market conditions, problems in the countries or regions they operate in, or for any number of other reasons – sometimes obscure and unexpected reasons.

Risk is notoriously difficult to identify, let alone quantify, and even so-called 'risk assessment experts' are often wrong in fact catastrophically wrong. As a case in point, US investment firm Long-Term Capital Management (LTCM), headed by two Nobel Prize-winning economists, made 40% per annum returns for their clients until their methods and risk management techniques failed spectacularly and without warning in 1998. LTCM's signature hedge fund lost $4.6 *billion* in four months in the wake of the Russian financial crisis. Clients were devastated and without a $3.625 billion bailout by the Federal Reserve Bank of New York the fallout would have cascaded through Wall Street and the global economy. Apparently nobody saw this 'Black Swan' event coming, and the risk management strategies of the founders, in which so much trust and money had been placed, were cast into disrepute. So, while it seems sensible that risk is to be avoided at all cost often neither you nor the so-called experts can even identify what the risks might be let alone avoid or mitigate them.

So What are the Types of Risk?

At the highest level there are known and unknown risks of a scale that could alter, perhaps irrevocably, the entire global economy, such as global climate change, ecosystem overload and loss of biodiversity, the threat of nuclear terrorism or war, a global pandemic of some sort, or the end of oil. These risks are difficult, perhaps impossible, to deal with and insure against in our current economic system, so if any or all come to fruition all bets are off on any investment system.

At a lower level and more easily grasped, though still very hard to predict and insure against, are 'geopolitical risks' such as volatility in the Middle East, dubious governance in Russia, conventional war or the potential for political meltdown in many Asian countries. Geopolitical risk can be highly unpredictable and very damaging. As an example, consider the possible impacts on the global economy, which has placed its bets on China retaining its stability and rising into an economic superpower, of civil unrest or perhaps even civil war and regime collapse in that country.

At the next level down are 'sector risks,' meaning risks within a specific sector of the economy, such as the impact of sub-prime mortgages on the banking and financial sector during the Credit Crunch of 2008. It could be risks in the consumer sector from high unemployment, or the resource sector from a sudden collapse in demand during recessionary periods in the economic cycle. Or it could be risks in the pharmaceutical and health sectors from drug patent expirations or regulatory changes or lawsuits. Ultimately, any sector is subject to turmoil caused by government policy changes, changes in demand for resources, financial meltdown or recession. When a sector tanks, often all companies in the sector get sucked down regardless of their quality as market sentiment turns against the sector.

At the lowest level are 'company-specific risks,' which, though generally limited to one company, unless they are large enough to affect an entire sector, can still have catastrophic impacts on even the oldest, largest and seemingly most stable companies. This is what happened to Barings Bank, which was the oldest merchant bank in London. Founded in 1762, it was the model of a solid, established company. Then in 1995 it went bust almost overnight because of unauthorized speculative trades by a Singapore-based Barings employee named Nick Leeson, enabled by poor management oversight. When his huge bets went very wrong, after 233 years of business, Barings went bankrupt.

Another obvious recent example of company-level risk is BP, one of the largest UK-based companies. In 2010, when its Deep Water Horizon drilling platform exploded and sank in the Gulf of Mexico, the company hit the rocks. Not only were many people killed on the platform, the subsequent well blow-out caused probably the worst oil spill in US history, widespread environmental damage and destroyed innumerable livelihoods along the US Gulf Coast. In the immediate aftermath, BP's share price dropped dramatically and the company suspended all dividend payments. There was even speculation that BP would be dismembered and sold off to other companies. Until the disaster, BP accounted for about 14% of all dividend payments made by companies in the FTSE 100 on the London Stock Exchange. It was a hundred-year-old giant, employing 80,000 people and operating in 100 countries, brought to its knees by a single accident. Had your entire portfolio consisted of BP shares, the portfolio would have suffered catastrophic capital loss at the same time that all dividend payment dried up.

At the personal level, there is also, as mentioned above, the risk of low returns. This is the risk not of losing your capital but that inaction or poor investment choices, such as holding your money in a bank savings account that pays less than inflation, will all but guarantee financial failure. Ironically, the traditional risk aversion of 'savers' who flock to the apparent safety of bank deposits and who would never go near a stock market for fear of loss is basically a long slow march towards poverty.

Lack of liquidity is another risk to any portfolio. Liquidity refers to how easily, quickly and cheaply an asset or investment can be converted into cash. A house, for example, is highly illiquid, meaning it can take many months to sell, it incurs a high commission charge and the final price is subject to local conditions of employment, demand and the ability of buyers to secure financing. Large-cap shares, on the other hand, are highly liquid, with millions changing hands daily, often thousands by the second, for just a single company. The price is highly transparent, purchase and sell orders are executed in milliseconds and the commission fees might only be $10–30 for thousands of dollars worth of shares. Much of my portfolio could be turned into cash in a dozen one-minute electronic transactions. Try that with a house that is dropping in value. In the age of financial turbulence and uncertainty, liquidity is king and needs to feature high on the list of desirable attributes of an investment portfolio.

When it comes to mitigating risk and selecting investments for the Child Millionaire portfolio, we can't easily do anything about the largest-scale risks as these would inherently alter the face of the global economy, perhaps rendering it unrecognizable. However, we will be looking to minimize the geopolitical, sector, company-specific and cyclical risks, and enhance exposure to growing Asian markets, to allow as high a return on our investment as possible and ensure liquidity, all at as low a cost as possible.

As with inflation, the point is that we can't predict many possible risks, so the best that we can do is to choose investments that mitigate as wide a range of potential risks as possible. This decreases the risk of failure and increases the chances that, within a range of probable outcomes, the Child Millionaire portfolio will be successful.

Let's turn now to the practicalities of setting up the Child Millionaire portfolio.

5

How to Setup a Child Millionaire Portfolio

Before we look at how to setup the Child Millionaire portfolio, let's review and summarize the Child Millionaire investment formula:

Shares in high quality dividend-paying companies + annual increase in dividend payout + annual appreciation in share price + automatic dividend reinvestment (compounding using automatic reinvestment) + monthly automatic contribution + lots of time = Child Millionaire, even after inflation.

So how do we build a Child Millionaire portfolio?

There are two basic ways to setup the Child Millionaire investment system.

- Use a discount online brokerage to purchase either Exchange Traded Funds (ETFs) or shares in individual companies.
- Purchase shares in individual companies directly and for free through a Share Purchase Plan (SPP) and have the dividends reinvested automatically and for free with a Dividend Reinvestment Plan (DRIP).

Let's look at the options in detail so you can gauge their suitability for you.

Using a Discount Online Brokerage to Manage the Child Millionaire Portfolio

The basic steps are as follows:

- Set your investment goal – e.g. do you want your child to have $1 million when they turn 20, 40, 60, etc. Use the Child Millionaire Calculator (see below) to figure how much you need to invest to achieve your goal.

- Check what tax-free investment accounts are available to you and your child.
- If available in your country, open a tax-free, low-fee investment account with a discount broker. If no tax-free account is available, set up a regular brokerage account and name it 'Child Millionaire Portfolio' so you and your child know what the goal is.
- Deposit an initial investment of as much as you can afford – $10,000, $1,000, $100 – or if you don't have a lump sum and the broker allows it, put in the minimum of $25–50 to start, and set up an automatic monthly withdrawal from your bank account for the sum required to achieve your goal as determined by the Child Millionaire Calculator.
- Have the brokerage account set up to automatically reinvest all dividends, if possible.
- Have the brokerage account set up to make automatic purchases of shares on a monthly or quarterly basis equal to the amount you are depositing in the account, if possible.
- Select your investments.
- Stop reading the financial press, forget about the account, let compounding and time do its work, and go have fun with your kids.

That's it. You have just minted a Child Millionaire.

Let's look at the steps in more detail.

Set Your Investment Goal

As with a road trip, if you don't have a destination in mind when you start, you won't know where you are going or how to get there. The same is true with investing. For the Child Millionaire system to work you need to set a goal. You can start by asking yourself at what age you would like your child to become a millionaire. Alternatively you can flip the question around and ask yourself how much money you would like the Child Millionaire portfolio to contain when your child turns 20, 40, 60, etc. What you desire and what is achievable will depend on your resources, namely how much money you have to invest now in a lump sum, if any, and how much you are able to commit on a monthly basis. It also depends on assumptions about rates of return and future inflation.

To allow you to experiment with all of the variables – your investment goal, share price, initial investment, reinvestment, share price appreciation, dividend yield and annual dividend growth rate – you can download the easy to use Child Millionaire Calculator from the 'calculator' tab at www.childmillionaire.com. The calculator is an Excel spreadsheet. The cells highlighted in red are the variables you can play around with to see the impact of different-sized initial or monthly contributions over various time frames. As guidance, the best dividend-paying companies with dividend growth aren't likely to be yielding more than 2.5–5.5% per annum, with annual appreciation of 3–5% and increases in dividends over time of 8–12% per annum, so don't delude yourself with outlandish assumptions. Be realistic.

Also, keep in mind that the Child Millionaire Calculator *does not* account for inflation, so the results are 'nominal' (see the earlier discussion on inflation). To figure out what the value of the portfolio and the quarterly dividend income will be in today's dollars or pounds if inflation averages 3.82% over time (or higher), you will need to divide the portfolio value and quarterly income numbers by the values in the right-hand column of the table below at the various year intervals in the left-hand column.

Converting 'nominal' values to the value in 'today's dollars/pounds'

Number of years	Divide 'nominal' portfolio value or dividend income by the following numbers to determine the equivalent value in today's dollars/pounds assuming long term inflation as follows			
	3.82% inflation	5% inflation	7.5% inflation	10% inflation
20	2.12	2.65	4.25	6.73
40	4.48	7.04	18.04	45.30
60	9.48	18.68	76.65	304.48
80	20.07	49.56	325.59	2,048.40

You may want to finish reading the rest of the book before you get too deeply into the projections, to make sure you understand what assumptions are reasonable.

Check What Tax-Free Investment Accounts are Available to You and Your Child

It is possible that in your country there is a tax-free account that could be used to hold and shelter investments. In the UK, such an account is called an Individual Savings Account (ISA) and for 2010–11 the ISA holder can contribute up to £10,200 per annum (about $16,000), set to increase to £10,680 in 2011–12 and by the Retail Price Index (RPI) per annum thereafter. In Canada, the equivalent is called a Tax Free Savings Account or TSFA. TSFAs were introduced in 2009 and each person is allowed to contribute $5,000 per year, which is set to increase to $5,500 in 2012. Unlike the ISA in the UK, with TSFAs any unused portion can be carried forward indefinitely. ISAs and TSFAs have unfortunate names because they lead many people to believe that they are only eligible for bank-style cash savings; in reality you can hold most mainstream shares, funds and bonds and other investments inside an ISA or TSFA. Once money is deposited into a tax-free ISA or TSFA account, any investment income from dividends or capital gains is accrued tax-free and can be withdrawn at any time without generating a tax liability. This is true even if the value of your account grows into the millions. Keep in mind, though, that money withdrawn cannot be replaced without cutting into your annual contribution allowance. Unfortunately, in the UK you have to be 16 years old to open a cash-deposit ISA, 18 for a shares-based ISA, and in Canada you have to be 18 to open a TSFA. These age restrictions preclude using these tax shelters to start your initial Child Millionaire portfolio. However, when your child turns the relevant age, he or she can start to transfer their portfolio into an ISA or TSFA, assuming such tax shelters still exist. The USA unfortunately doesn't have an ISA/TSFA direct equivalent. The closest thing is a Roth IRA, though with a Roth IRA money can't be withdrawn until the owner is 59.5 years old, which, as I'll explain later, isn't ideal.

In the UK, there used to be a tax shelter called a 'Child Trust Fund,' which was eliminated in 2010. A proposed 'Junior ISA' is slated to be implemented in autumn 2011. Although the details aren't yet known, it seems likely that parents and friends will be able to contribute up to £1,200 per year into the fund, which will be held in the child's name until he or she turns 18, at which point it can be rolled into a normal ISA. Any investment income or capital gains earned within the 'Junior ISA' would accrue tax-free. Once the Junior ISA is available, this should be the vehicle of choice for UK parents building a Child Millionaire portfolio.

In the meantime, while waiting for your child to be eligible for a tax shelter, if you have space in your ISA or TSFA, you should consider starting your portfolio in one of these tax shelters.

Open a Tax-Free, Low-Fee Investment Account with a Discount Broker

If you don't have access to, or space in, existing tax shelters, then simply open a regular non-registered account with a discount broker that has electronic (online) trading. Make sure that the broker allows you to purchase shares in the US markets if you live in the UK or Canada or elsewhere. Preferably the broker should also allow you to make automatic monthly deposits into your brokerage account from your bank account.

The impact of brokerage fees – commissions on share purchases and sales, annual 'management' or 'inactivity' fees – can be quite dramatic and must be avoided at all costs. Look for a broker with low-commission fees, low or no annual management fees, and above all one that offers dividend reinvestment at zero commission and low or zero commission for regular contributions. I recommend checking out TD Waterhouse for Canada, the UK and the US.

Deposit an Initial Investment of as Much as You Can Afford

Deposit your initial investment, or if the broker allows it put in the minimum to start (usually $25–50), and set up an automatic monthly withdrawal from your bank account for the amount determined by the goal you have set by experimenting with the Child Millionaire Calculator. If you can swing it, start with $5,000 or £5,000 and monthly contributions of $100 or £100 or more. If you are using a UK Junior ISA you will probably be limited to only £1,200 per year, so if you want to contribute more you may have to hold part of the Child Millionaire portfolio outside of the Junior ISA.

Keep in mind that you can easily change the monthly amount if your circumstances change and also make one-off deposits of money from relatives. The important thing is to get started even if you only have $50.

Have the Brokerage Account Set Up to Automatically Reinvest All Dividends

Many brokerage accounts enable dividends to be reinvested at a lower-than-normal commission rate (this is sometimes called a 'synthetic dividend reinvestment plan' or 'synthetic DRIP'). It is important not to be paying full commission to reinvest dividends as this will destroy your portfolio growth. For example, in our fictional portfolio, if we are earning $62.50 per quarter in dividends and the brokerage commission to purchase additional shares is $30, then the cost per transaction would consume almost half of the return and thus greatly undermine the compounding.

Consequently, if you are only contributing a relatively small amount of money per month, it would be better to accumulate the dividends and the regular monthly contributions, and purchase additional shares only once or twice a year to spread the commission charge over a larger purchase. The downside is that this diminishes the dollar cost averaging advantage and allows for emotion or laziness to creep in. Also, through brokers you can only purchase whole shares, not fractions of a share, so you'd need to wait until you have sufficient money to purchase whole shares before placing a share purchase order. There is a way around this issue of fractional shares and the punitive cost of commissions, which I will discuss in the section on DRIP investing.

Have the Brokerage Account Set Up to Make Automatic Purchases of Shares on a Monthly or Quarterly Basis Equal to the Amount You are Depositing in the Account

Again, if you can't do this or you need to wait until you have sufficient cash in the account to make it worthwhile from a commission charge point of view, then schedule a quarterly reminder into your diary, mobile/cell phone or email software.

Select Your Investments

Once you have your Child Millionaire brokerage account setup you need to decide what to put in it. I'm going to discuss two options.

Option 1 involves purchasing Exchange Traded Funds (ETFs), which I'll explain in detail in the next chapter. Characteristics of an ETF-based approach include the following:

- It is best suited to those who have little investing knowledge and little interest in learning about investing, or those who are just plain lazy.
- It reduces company specific risk and often sector risk if a broad-based index ETF is chosen.
- It results in returns that are close to the overall stock market return and thus potentially much lower than for a Child Millionaire comprised of individual shares.

Option 2 involves purchasing shares in individual companies. Some characteristics of this system are as follows:

- It is for those who feel comfortable researching and selecting individual companies.
- It carries a high level of company-specific risk and sector risk if your shares are concentrated in a small number of companies and/or sectors.
- It results in returns (or losses) that are potentially much greater than the overall market return, in some cases an order of magnitude greater.
- It has a variation known as DRIP investing that allows the portfolio to be completely 'hands off' and incurs no commissions or management fees.

It is possible to combine Options 1 and 2 by building a portfolio that contains both ETFs and individual shares, to provide greater risk protection and potentially greater returns. Many investors start with ETFs and, as their investment knowledge grows, they add shares in individual companies.

Let's look at each option in detail.

6

Investing with ETFs – The Cheap (and Lazy) Answer

You now have the Child Millionaire portfolio brokerage account setup and ready to go, and you are ready to put some investments into it. Let's assume you are fairly risk-averse or not that interested in reading about companies and selecting shares. Or perhaps you are just lazy and simply want to get this system going so you can go back to napping. How can you minimize risk and yet select a high-quality investment that ticks most of the Child Millionaire portfolio boxes?

Mutual or unit trust funds advisors would tell you that they have the answer. Most mutual funds claim to provide expertise in investment selection and the ability to reduce company-specific or sector risk because their funds spread your money, and that of thousands of others, across dozens or hundreds of companies, often across many sectors and countries. This risk-spreading concept has a great deal going for it, as we will see. However, what cripples mutual funds and makes them worth avoiding are their poor average performance and high management fees, paid out of your capital, regardless of whether the fund gains or loses money in a given year. But what if we could combine the diversification and risk-spreading profile of a mutual fund with the liquidity and low management cost of an individual company's shares? We may well have the perfect investment vehicle.

These investments exist and are called Exchange Traded Funds (ETFs). ETFs are a bit like mutual funds or unit trusts in that they pool the money of thousands of individual and institutional investors and then use their size to invest across a wide selection of companies within a sector, or even within the market as a whole. However, this is where mutual funds or unit trusts and ETFs diverge dramatically.

A typical mutual fund needs to be purchased through a fund broker and, though reasonably liquid, purchases and sales can take days to settle. However, this isn't their main problem. Their main failing is the enormous management fees the funds charge. Fees can range from 1–3% or more (Canadian mutual funds in particular have very high fees) of the fund's annual value. This fee is paid *regardless* of how the fund performs. So, for example, if a fund lost 25% of its value in 2008 but it had a Management Expense Ratio (MER) of 2.5%, then the fund managers would withdraw 2.5% of the capital of the fund as their fee even though the fund lost money, so the investors would be down even more.

Some mutual funds also charge a fixed percentage of your capital for entry – called a 'front load' – which can be as much as 5% or your capital. Some charge an exit fee called a 'back load' which is a percentage of your total capital if you sell out of the fund. The effect of management fees on the overall performance of a portfolio is massive. Given that up to 80% of all mutual funds actually *underperform* their stock market benchmark, partially because of the draining effect of high fees, fund mangers are effectively being paid huge fees from investors' money to do a very, very poor job.

ETFs, on the other hand, trade on the large stock exchanges just like a regular stock, so they can be bought and sold in seconds at low commission rates and they are highly liquid. Although they pool money, ETFs are designed to track various sectors, investment themes or entire stock market indices, and thus there is little, if any, human stock-picking prowess or folly involved. ETF managers do this by purchasing a selection and proportion of stocks that matches those tracked by a given index such as the FTSE 100 or S&P 500. This means that the cost of running an ETF is very low because there is little research, work and management compared to an 'actively managed' mutual fund. This low cost is reflected in the very low annual management fees, referred to as 'Total Expense Ratio' or 'TER', which are generally 0.2–0.65% per annum.

How ETFs Perform

Over the past few years ETFs have taken the markets by storm and there is now an ETF covering almost every conceivable market, sector and investment theme. One key aspect of ETFs is that, because they track various indices, they can't underperform their index (with the exception of the small impact of fees), but they also can't outperform their index. They simply track it. This means that you could lose out on the potentially larger gains possible by picking top stocks as investment legends like Warren Buffett or George Soros do. On the flipside you massively reduce company-specific and sector-specific risk, and the reality is that most people, professionals included, are horrible stock pickers. For the average investor building a Millionaire Child portfolio who has time on his side and who would rather be out playing football than pouring over corporate annual reports, analysing profit and loss sheets and trying to pick winning stocks, ETFs can seem a gift from the investing gods.

But how do they perform?

ETF performance depends largely on what index the ETF is tracking, and how well the index performs depends on how well the individual companies (shares) within the index perform. As an example, let's look at the Russell 3000 Index Fund provided by iShares, which is the leading supplier of ETFs. The fund was setup in May 2000, so there is about a decade of data available. The Russell 3000 index tracks the yield and share price performance of the broad US equity markets so it is a fairly good proxy for the performance of the entire US equity markets over the 2001–2010 period. This period is one that has seen a great deal of volatility, kicking off with the dotcom crash before spiking in the mid-2000s and then crashing again during the 2008 global financial crisis before rebounding to 2010.

Below are the annual returns of the ETF from 2001–2010, compared to the Russell 3000 index, which shows just how volatile this decade was. The difference between the ETF return and the index is accounted for by the management fee of 0.21% and the cost and churn of rebalancing the fund.

Performance of the Russell 3000 Index Fund ETF versus the index, 2001–10

Year	ETF return	Russell 3000 index return
2001	−11.78%	−11.46%
2002	−21.63%	−21.54%
2003	30.77%	31.06%
2004	11.76%	11.95%
2005	5.98%	6.12%
2006	15.52%	15.72%
2007	5.04%	5.14%
2008	−37.30%	−37.31%
2009	28.20%	28.34%
2010	16.75%	16.93%

Source: http://us.ishares.com/product_info/fund/performance/IWV.htm

As a point of comparison, how did 'dividend aristocrat' Johnson & Johnson and my old nemesis Nortel Networks perform during the same period? Let's assume that you bought $1,000 of each of the Russell 3000 Index Fund, Johnson & Johnson and Nortel Networks shares on 22 May 2000 when the fund was launched and you reinvested all dividends. Where would you be at the end of 2 Feb 2011?

Total return on $1,000 from 22 May 2000 to 2 February 2011, dividends reinvested

	Russell 3000 Index Fund ETF	Russell 3000 index	J&J shares	Nortel Networks shares
% return	1.47%	1.63%	70.89%	−99.9985%
Value	$1,014.70	$1,016.30	$1,709.75	$0 stock delisted in 2009

The poor results for the ETF illustrate a few points. Firstly, volatility over a relatively short period of time such as a decade can be deadly and years of great gain can be undone rapidly by years of great loss. This volatility is smoothed out over long time periods. Secondly, as mentioned before, an index tracker inherently includes all stocks in the index, so you take the 'dividend aristocrats' – companies that have a long history of paying and increasing dividends year after year (of which there are a large number in the Russell 3000 index tracking ETF) – along with the large number of dogs that don't increase dividends annually, or even stop paying them and lose value. The ETF share mix of the good, the bad and the ugly can severely hamper the results. Finally, the right company (J&J) can dramatically outperform the index just as choosing the wrong company (Nortel) can devastate the portfolio. So as a counterpoint to Johnson & Johnson's outperformance, over the same period Nortel Networks would have surged through an all-time high of C$124.50 per share by August 2000 before plummeting 99.9985% to a share price of C$0.185 in 2009 when the company was delisted from the TSX, resulting in a total loss of capital. The ETF achieves something in the middle – neither outstanding performance nor catastrophe.

Projecting ETF Returns Using Historical Figures

So do poor ETF returns from the past decade mean that index-tracking ETFs are a waste of time? Not necessarily, because with the Child Millionaire portfolio we have the advantage of a long time horizon. Because of the volatility of the past ten years, an index-tracking ETF is subject to the gyrations of the index that it broadly tracks. However, given that the Child Millionaire portfolio is inherently long-term – 20, 40, 60+ years – we can to some degree ignore the short term period of even ten years and look at the market return over a much longer period of time. Since ETFs haven't really been around much longer than ten of fifteen years, we need a proxy for longer-term performance. Since the ETF more or less mirrors the market then we might anticipate that it would perform similarly to the US market, which has a 141 year 'compound annual growth rate' (CAGR) or actual return including dividend reinvestment of 8.92% (versus the often-quoted higher 'average return' figure of 10.62%). The CAGR after adjustment for inflation is 6.72% (compared to the higher 'annual return' figure of 8.42%). As much as the past is or isn't a guide to the future, we could expect that over time an ETF tracker might be reasonably close to this long term average of 8.92% before/6.72% after inflation.

Disaggregating the S&P 500 historical returns to show how much return was provided by share appreciation, dividend yield and dividend yield growth gives slightly different figures depending on the timeframe chosen and how the results are calculated. Reasonable historical figures to plug into the Child Millionaire Calculator to simulate how an S&P 500 ETF *might* perform if all dividends are reinvested (excluding the impact of tax and fees) are as follows:

- The average yield for the S&P 500 from 1871–2007 was 4.5% per annum.
- The long term S&P 500 dividend growth rate from 1871–2007 was 3.47% per annum (the 1952–2007 rate is a higher 5.38% per annum).
- The annual share price appreciation for the S&P 500 (excluding dividends) for the 83 years from 1926–2009 was 6.98%.

Generally speaking, post-1950 returns are higher on average because they exclude the 1930s Great Depression and include the post-World War II rebuilding boom. For the sake of our modelling let's stick with the more conservative lower figures.

On this basis, it is reasonable to anticipate that over a long Child Millionaire timeframe a portfolio with an initial investment of $1,000 and $100 per month continuing for the duration in an S&P index-tracking, dividend-paying ETF with all dividends reinvested might look as follows.

Assumptions: $1,000 initial investment and $100 monthly contribution for the duration not increased by the rate of inflation, yield of 4.5%, dividend growth rate of 3.47% and annual stock price appreciation of 6.98% for an S&P 500 index tracker, all dividends reinvested, excluding impact of tax and management fees.

End of year	Nominal value (inflation not accounted for)	Portfolio value in purchasing power equivalent to today, i.e. accounting for inflation at 3.82%
1	$2,260	$2,177
20	$74,254	$35,025
40	$425,409	$94,957
60	$1,835,224	$193,589

Naturally different inputs give you different outputs so if you use the higher post-1952 dividend growth rate of 5.38% but leave everything else the same then the results would look even more impressive.

End of year	Nominal value (inflation not accounted for)	Portfolio value in purchasing power equivalent to today, i.e. accounting for inflation at 3.82%
1	$2,260	$2,177
20	$82,243	$38,794
40	$620,989	$138,614
60	$3,895,100	$410,876

The differences in the above outcomes illustrates the difficulties in projecting future values based on past results, especially when the long-term past results vary depending on the sample selected and when the future is inherently unknown. Nevertheless, the above range of outcomes *probably* suggests more likely future long-term returns on an S&P 500 ETF than would projections based on the figures from the past decade, because the volatility has been smoothed out by averages.

'Distributed' versus 'Accumulating' ETFs

Some dividend ETFs have automatic dividend reinvestment built into them. When researching ETFs online, on the fact sheet for the ETF under 'Use of Income,' you will see either 'Distributed' or 'Accumulating,' sometimes called 'Reinvestment'. 'Distributed' means that the dividends paid into the ETF by the stocks held in the ETF are paid out to unit holders (shareholders) of the ETF on a regular quarterly, semi-annual or annual basis. These dividends will be accumulated in cash in your brokerage account and you will need to reinvest them manually in the ETF to ensure compounding, preferably with additional money from your regular contributions to amortize the commission charge over a larger purchase.

When an ETF uses income for 'Accumulating' this means that your portion of the income (dividends) from the underlying stocks in the ETF isn't paid out to you in cash but rather is retained within the ETF and used by the fund manager to purchase additional shares in companies held in the ETF.

I'd normally opt for the most automatic form of reinvestment – i.e. accumulation – however, in most tax jurisdictions there is a significant difference how the two different types of income are treated. Tax law changes frequently, so you should read the ETF company information on how ETF income is treated for tax purposes for the funds you are choosing in your tax jurisdiction.

In the UK, for example, income that is distributed to unit holders from an equity (shares) ETF as cash is generally treated as 'dividend income.' Dividend income is the lowest-taxed income in most jurisdictions, as opposed to, say, interest income, which can be amongst the highest taxed. So an investor in the basic UK tax rate category, meaning someone who earns less than £37,400 in tax year 2010–11, pays only 10% tax on dividend income, which is automatically deducted by the fund as a 'dividend tax credit' before distribution to the fund unit holder. In the USA and Canada the numbers for dividend tax are slightly different, but overall relatively similar in that generally speaking dividends are among the lowest taxed-forms of income. It is well worth reading up on the basics of your tax jurisdiction and/or checking with a tax expert with respect to dividend income.

With ETFs that automatically reinvest or 'accumulate' the dividends within the fund the income is treated differently depending on the jurisdiction. For example, for a UK tax payer, the income on an 'Accumulating' iShares ETF, which is 'domiciled' – i.e. held and managed in Ireland – is retained within the fund and tax isn't paid on this income. However, if the funds are sold by you then the capital gain on the sales is taxed as 'offshore income gains' and is thus subject to the full marginal income tax rate of 40-50% rather than the much lower 18% tax for regular capital gains after the basic annual capital gains exemption. It's hard to calculate the impact of this different tax structure over time, not least because the tax rules are constantly changing. I strongly suggest that you read the information sheets from the ETF provider you are considering to see how income is treated and seek expert tax advice if you need to before making a decision on whether to invest in an ETF that distributes income or one that accumulates income. Sorting out the tax issues beforehand is absolutely vital to ensuring that you don't pay too much tax now or create a future 'tax bomb' that decimates the Child Millionaire portfolio.

Liquidity, Diversification and Fees

Overall, for the liquidity and diversification they offer, the low management fees of 0.3–0.65% on ETFs are good value. If you ever need to liquidate the portfolio it's as simple as placing a stock sell order through your online broker, which takes less than a minute, and your portfolio will be converted to cash for only the price of a regular commission of $10–30.

The Downside of ETFs

Naturally, one downside of ETFs is the management fee, as any management fee, no matter how small, presents a headwind to returns. Another detractor mentioned above is that because of management fees and the fact that ETFs need to constantly rebalance their holdings to reflect the index they track, this churn creates transaction costs, which also creates a subtle drain on the compounding that you don't experience with individual shares. Over time, the effect of even very low management fees and rebalancing costs means that ETFs tend to shadow their index but underperform by a small amount.

The final downside of ETFs is the flipside of the benefits of diversification discussed above, which is that because ETFs track an index, they inherently can't outperform the index, but neither can they underperform it except by the small effect of management fees and churn. As we saw in the example above of the Russell

3000 tracker ETF versus Johnson & Johnson, if chosen well, individual shares can outperform the index, sometimes dramatically, just as they can sometimes perform dramatically worse than the index, as in the case of Nortel Networks. ETFs always do exactly what the broader index does, so as a trade-off they offer diversification but 'average' index performance versus the 'outperformance,' on the upside or the downside, offered by individual shares. For many investors, the benefits of ETFs outweigh the downsides. Only you can decide, but if you don't have the inclination or time to research individual companies, nor the somewhat greater appetite for risk needed to invest in individual shares, then on balance you are better off sticking with ETFs and using the long-term rates of return for the market as a whole for your Child Millionaire portfolio projections.

Choosing ETFs

If you are going to opt for an ETF-based portfolio, then I'd suggest that you start with only one, possibly two ETFs for your Child Millionaire portfolio, which can be added to as the portfolio grows in size. Fewer ETFs means you can buy more units in a single ETF with the regular monthly or quarterly contribution and dividend reinvestment, which will lower your commission charges and boost your return.

A good place to get started with ETFs is iShares, which is the world's leading provider of ETFs. iShares ETFs (or a comparable ETF provider) should all be available for purchase through any decent online brokerage. As a first initial 'core' part of your Child Millionaire portfolio I'd consider an ETF that tracks one or more major indexes – the Dow, the S&P 500, or the Russell 3000 (a broad measure of US markets), the FTSE 100 or the TSX Composite Index – probably starting with the index in your home country.

Don't be put off by the sheer variety and overwhelming selection of ETFs. Zero straight in on the developed economy ETFs tracking one of these major indexes and have a read of the fund information sheet, which will detail the management fee (TER) percentage. On fees, lower is always better for performance – in the 0.3% range is good but don't sweat an extra 0.1 or 0.2%. Check whether there are any other costs or fees, which there shouldn't be, and check the underlying yield, noting that a higher yield is generally better.

An example of such an ETF for UK investors who want to track the FTSE 100 is the iShares FTSE 100. This ETF has a Total Expense Ratio (TER) of 0.4%, which is pretty low and thus good, and the underlying yield (when I checked) was 2.73%, which is decent but not amazing. Above 4% would be better. Keep in mind that the yield will change as the value of the underlying shares in the FTSE 100 change. If the FTSE 100 drops, the yield will increase, and if the FTSE 100 increases in value the yield will decrease. This fluctuation is where your regular contributions to the Child Millionaire portfolio and dollar/pound cost averaging come into play. When the market is high you will purchase fewer units in the fund and when the market is low you will purchase more units.

Because the FTSE 100 is heavily weighted towards mining, oil, large pharmaceuticals and financial companies that have exposure to the rapidly growing economies of Asia, by holding this ETF you will benefit to some degree from the Asian boom, but not as much as if you had invested in an Asian-focused ETF. Correspondingly, however, you are not exposed to the potential for catastrophic market loss in one geographic area such as Asia, which, all things considered, is still a pretty precarious place to invest.

Another option might be a higher-yield dividend-focused ETF such as the iShares FTSE Dividend Plus, which yields about 4.5% and which tracks a selection of higher-yielding FTSE shares from companies that may not be in the FTSE 100 but that pay high dividend yields. On the US markets you might also look at iShares as well as SPDR's Dividend Aristocrats S&P ETF, which as its name suggests, focuses on the US dividend aristocrats. Rest assured that no matter where you live there is an ETF that will suit you, be it an S&P 500, Dow, TSX or FTSE tracker, or one that tracks European dividend-paying companies.

Just remember the key principles:

- The ETF should track an index comprised of high-quality, large dividend-paying companies.
- The expense ratio (TER) should be low (0.2–0.65% maximum).
- There should be no other costs involved in purchasing, selling or owning except your broker's commission.
- Preferably the fund distributes income.
- The fund should be diversified enough – i.e. the index it tracks is geographically dispersed in terms of the types of companies held and sectors covered – that you get exposure to developed-country stability, plus Asian or emerging-market growth, while reducing the overall risk that would come with a geographically or sector-specific ETF.

- You must regularly reinvest the dividends in more units no matter what the overall market is doing.

An ETF tracking any large stock market index should fit the bill nicely.

How to Buy ETFs through an Online Broker

Once you have chosen your ETF you need to make your initial online investment through your brokerage account. The brokerage account needs to have sufficient money in it to cover the value of the ETF units you are purchasing plus the commission charge from your broker, which will vary by broker and country. For a purchase of a few thousand dollars or pounds it shouldn't be more than $10–30 or £10–20.

Buying an ETF is as easy as placing a purchase order for the ETF ticker symbol, which you can find on the ETF supplier's website – for example the ticker for the iShares FTSE 100 is 'ISF' – through your online broker account, entering the number of units you want to buy and clicking on the appropriate buttons. You should receive a confirmation and your ETF units will show up within a day or so, often instantaneously, in your online account, and you are up and running.

Make it Automatic

The next thing to do if you haven't already done so is to setup an automatic monthly withdrawal from your bank account into the Child Millionaire brokerage account. Quarterly dividend payments for the ETF units you bought initially will automatically be paid into your brokerage account. Next – and this is *key* to the success of the entire plan – in order to take advantage of compounding and dollar/pound cost averaging you *must* reinvest both the dividend income distributions from the ETF and your regular monthly cash contributions into more ETF units on a regular basis. You need to do this religiously, regardless of what the overall market is doing or the Child Millionaire plan won't work. Since you want to spread the broker's commission charge for any ETF purchase over as large a purchase as possible, you should invest only when you've accumulated several hundred dollars or pounds, preferably more, but *no less than* quarterly or you will lose the advantage of dollar/pound cost averaging. If you can setup a very low-cost (such as that offered by TD Waterhouse) or free automatic dividend reinvestment and purchase plan with your broker then do so, however, be sure to check what fees you will need to pay, if any. If your broker charges you a full purchase commission each time dividends are reinvested then your money will be eroded very quickly, and it would be better to accumulate more and manually reinvest it to spread the commission charges, and/or look for a cheaper broker.

In the absence of an automatic reinvestment plan you shouldn't rely on your memory to make the regular purchases. You will undoubtedly get sidetracked, forget or worse, get swayed by media coverage of market volatility and then get sucked into trying to time the market, which you definitely want to avoid in favour of benefiting from dollar/pound cost averaging. To help with this, set yourself a reminder in your diary and make the purchase every 3 or 6 months regardless of what the market is doing and *never* be tempted to sell your holdings if the market drops as you will defeat the entire purpose of the system. The Child Millionaire portfolio is long-term so try to think like someone investing for 40 or 60 years into the future, not the next quarter, year or even decade. Be stoic, or better yet ignore the market and just keep buying, quarter after quarter, year after year, decade after decade.

Over Time, Diversify into Sectors

Although a broad index-based ETF would already be diversified across most sectors, over time you might decide to add a second or third or fourth ETF to the Child Millionaire portfolio, to focus on a more specific geographic region or an industry such as healthcare. However, the same principles apply as before. Only purchase an ETF that tracks the leading index of top-quality dividend-paying companies within the geographic region or sector. No pure growth plays or speculative bets on the mining sector or penny stocks. The Child Millionaire is about investing, not speculating; the latter is an activity akin to gambling and comes with all the traps of market timing, emotion, turmoil and potential for catastrophic loss. Keep in mind that adding more ETFs increases your commission fees for investing and dividend reinvestment so make sure it is worth it. Finally, remember that above all the Child Millionaire portfolio has the advantage of huge amounts of time, so invest regularly and let the portfolio take care of itself.

7

Investing in Individual Company Shares

Building a Child Millionaire portfolio of individual shares follows largely the same steps as building a portfolio with ETFs, the difference being what investments go into the portfolio. In this chapter I'll take you through how to build a Child Millionaire portfolio from a selection of individual shares. Then in the next chapter I'll explain a technique for building an all-shares portfolio. While slightly more complicated and time consuming to setup, once up and running this is possibly the easiest and cheapest system. In fact this system can be setup for $50–100 and you will never have to pay another penny in commissions or fees, which will have a dramatic positive effect on the Child Millionaire portfolio.

The main upside of a Child Millionaire portfolio of individual shares is that a selection of the right 'dividend aristocrat' shares can dramatically outperform an ETF portfolio, as we saw in the last chapter with J&J versus the Russell 3000 Index ETF. The downside of a portfolio of individual shares is the lack of diversification and the substantial company-specific and sector-specific risk if you start with only 1–4 companies, even if these are top-quality companies. Company-specific risk, which is generally reasonably high even for large, old companies (if you doubt this then think of BP or Barings), can be reduced over time for the Child Millionaire portfolio as a whole through greater diversification into the shares of more companies – perhaps up to 15 or 20.

Add Individual Shares to the ETF-based Child Millionaire Portfolio

The most straightforward and lowest-risk way of amplifying the potential return of the Child Millionaire portfolio is to augment a primary ETF holding that comprises, say, 40–80% of your portfolio value with share holdings in individual companies. The diversified ETF forms a base, and the individual stocks allow greater focus in specific sectors and individual winning shares. With this system, on a quarterly basis, you could deliberately choose to reinvest the dividends from the ETFs into specific shares. For example, if your Child Millionaire portfolio contains one broad index-tracking ETF and shares in four companies, you could channel all of the dividend reinvestment money into the one or two companies in your portfolio that have seen the *greatest drop* or *least increase* in share price to maximize the power of dollar/pound cost averaging. This is a powerful compounding strategy.

If you decide to add individual shares to your Child Millionaire portfolio then it is worth bearing in mind that probably 90%+ of company shares on the various markets (including those tracked by most ETFs) aren't worth owning individually. The only companies worth considering for Child Millionaire portfolio are so-called 'dividend aristocrats,' which have the following attributes:

- They are the leaders in their sectors. This might mean, but not necessarily, that a company is the largest in its sector so it has size, pricing power and market advantage.
- The company isn't, as far as you can tell, subject to substantial risk from a single catastrophic event such as what happened to BP in 2010.
- The company pays a large dividend that amounts to a high yield of at least 2.5%, preferably closer to 5%, and it does this while paying out *less than* 75% of its profits as dividends. Very high-yielding shares i.e., 6.50%+, should generally be avoided because a very high yield is usually unsustainable. You can check this on Yahoo Finance, Google Finance, Bloomberg, Stockhouse or any number of other financial websites.
- The company has a long meaning 10+, but preferably 25+ year, track record of *increasing the dividend amount* year after year. To check this look at dividend aristocrat lists or the dividend history in the investor relations part of the company's website.
- The company is growing, meaning its income, profit and share price are increasing over time. Again, you can check this out on any financial website.

Dividend Aristocrats

Most dividend aristocrats are American and are listed on the NYSE. The S&P 500 Dividend Aristocrat list is the obvious place to start your search. Another source is the list at Seeking Alpha. Or you can just Google 'dividend aristocrats' with your country name and go from there.

The S&P Dividend Aristocrats list only includes companies that have increased their dividends for at least 25 consecutive years. If companies stop increasing their dividend or, worse, stop paying it they are dropped from the list. Companies on the list include many familiar names, such as Coca Cola, Johnson & Johnson, 3M, Kimberly-Clark, Proctor and Gamble and others that are usually giants within their sectors and also globally. This gives them geographic diversification and exposure to growth in Asia and elsewhere.

Johnson & Johnson, for example, is one of the world leaders in healthcare products. The company owns hundreds of brands and some 70% of J&J's revenue is derived from products that are either in first or second position in their sector worldwide. The company has a market capitalization of about $170 billion dollars and operates in almost every country in the world. As of 2010 earnings per share and the annual dividend had been hiked for the past 48 years making this company a giant in all respects. As Western populations age and Asian countries become wealthier, global spending on healthcare products is also increasing, and J&J stands to benefit tremendously from its pole position in the sector. There are others with similar stature in their respective fields on the list and all are worth considering for your portfolio.

In Canada, and to a lesser extent the UK, dividend aristocrats are harder to find because these countries' economies are smaller and often less diversified than the US. If you have a brokerage account that allows you to purchase on the NYSE then you can easily add US-based Dividend Aristocrats to your portfolio. Bear in mind that tax laws in the US mean that you may be sent some paperwork by your brokerage and some tax on dividends may be withheld from your dividend payment automatically by the US Internal Revenue Service (IRS). This shouldn't deter you from owning S&P 500 Dividend Aristocrats, but it's worth thinking about.

In Canada, the selection of dividend aristocrat-like companies is smaller and historically tends to be focused on resource-related companies and banks. Options can be found on the Standard and Poors website. Recently many banks have been dropped from lists because of a freeze on dividend increases, though all are still paying healthy dividends. Canadian banks are large, generally well-regulated and fairly conservative, though not necessarily as well-regulated or conservative as Canadian media tends to suggest.

Still, Canadian banks have an unparalleled track record of paying dividends. Royal Bank has been paying for 140 years, bank of Montreal for 181 years, CIBC for 142 years, TD, which owns the TD Waterhouse brokerage, for 153 years and the Bank of Nova Scotia (Scotia Bank) for 177 years. Most of these banks have been paying dividends longer than Canada has been an independent country. Furthermore, many had a track record of dividend increases spanning decades, until the recent global economic crisis. All of this being said, Canadian banks are heavily exposed to the domestic real estate market, which has reached all-time highs and is looking very precarious, so it may be best to wait a bit on these to see what happens to the property market and the banks over the next couple of years.

One Canadian company worth considering, but not the only one, is Enbridge, which owns some of the major natural gas and oil pipelines in Canada and the US. Unlike resource companies whose profits swing with the price of oil or gas, Enbridge is in the business of moving oil and gas regardless of its underlying price. Pipelines are expensive to build, so Enbridge has a powerful advantage over upstart rivals, pipelines tend to pay on multi-year contracts and the infrastructure lasts for decades. Furthermore, Enbridge has been paying dividends for about 60 years and has a strong history of prioritizing dividend growth. At the end of 2010 the dividend was increased by 15%, and the company's future growth plans and focus on paying investor dividends suggests this pattern will continue making it a company well-worth considering.

In the UK, companies worth considering include utilities and energy suppliers such as Scottish and Southern Energy or National Grid, which, like Enbridge, owns the means of energy transmission as well as pharmaceutical giants such as GlaxoSmithKline. The S&P Dividend Aristocrats for Europe (including the UK) is a good starting point for research as is a list at investment website the Motley Fool. Another good starting point for finding dividend aristocrats is the *Financial Times* FT30 list, which contains many of the largest and most stable dividend payers from across the full swathe of the UK economy. Those looking for exposure to Asia should look more widely at the FTSE 100 as the FT30 is quite UK-focused.

Buying Individual Shares

When adding individual shares to the Child Millionaire portfolio, as with ETFs, you simply place the share order through your online brokerage account using the company stock ticker code and pay the commission. For example, Scottish and Southern Energy's ticker on the London Stock Exchange (LSE) is 'SSE.' The shares will be added to the portfolio and dividend payments will be paid into the account on a regular basis.

As with ETFs, these dividends and your regular contributions *must* be reinvested on a regular basis to take advantage of dollar/pound cost averaging and the compound effect. The biggest advantage of individual shares is that you can pick the biggest, most successful companies in a sector – i.e. the Johnson & Johnsons – which over the long term will tend to outperform the index and index-tracking ETFs. On the flipside, as mentioned before, the biggest danger of owning individual stocks is 'individual company risk.' With more of your eggs in one company's basket rather than spread across, say, the 100 companies of the FTSE 100 or the 500 companies of the S&P 500, your risk increases dramatically.

Risk and Diversification

Imagine you have your Child Millionaire portfolio in only two companies, one of which is XYZ Company. Imagine that next year XYZ Company has a catastrophic, yet perhaps unpredictable incident such as BP faced with the Deep Water Horizon explosion and it loses 70% of its value. Your portfolio, if invested equally in only the two companies, would experience an overall 35% capital loss, which could be even worse if your other company holding is in the same economic sector as XYZ Company and suffers some 'contagion' effect. If, however, your portfolio is invested in a FTSE 100 ETF and XYZ Company comprises 1% of the ETF when it loses 70% of its value, then the loss to your Child Millionaire portfolio would only be 0.3%, which is relatively inconsequential.

Individual company stocks can dramatically increase the risk to your portfolio, however, this risk can be mitigated to a significant extent by the following:

- Investing in at least five companies across different sectors (healthcare, financial/banking, energy, consumer staples, telecommunications) and over time expanding this to include up to 20 companies spread across different sectors. If you have a large core holding of ETFs in the Child Millionaire portfolio you can get away with shares in fewer companies.
- Choosing companies that are leaders in their sectors and that operate across dozens, perhaps hundreds of countries to mitigate country or regionally specific political and currency risk.

- Choosing dividend aristocrats. Although the past doesn't foretell the future, the momentum to keep paying and raising dividends is very strong for companies whose reputations ride on it.
- Choosing companies that have a low-risk business model – i.e. Johnson & Johnson sells hundreds of products across hundreds of markets, so a single 'product failure' would have a small impact on the company overall compared to the impact of the explosion of BP's Deep Water Horizon.
- Choosing companies in sectors that are growing and catering to Asian and other emerging markets.
- Choosing companies in non-cyclical and non-discretionary industries – i.e. companies that produce things people need to buy regardless of the state of the economic cycle, such as drugs and healthcare products, household products, toilet paper, electricity, etc.
- Choosing companies whose business model you could explain to a 10-year old, i.e. 'ABC Company makes product x which they sell to people who need something that does y' (think of toilet paper, or dish soap) *not* 'EFG Company leverages global currency arbitrage to provide novel financial products to innovative lenders servicing highly leveraged borrowers building venture capital portfolios of biotechnology technology companies in the Indian market.'
- Choosing companies that aren't highly leveraged i.e. not built upon excessive borrowing and subject to non-linear, scalable events such as the global Credit Crunch, which bankrupted or nearly bankrupted (had governments not intervened) highly exposed and leveraged companies like Lehman Brothers and various Icelandic, Irish, Dutch, UK and US banks.
- Choosing companies that have a technical, brand or other market advantage – sometimes called a 'moat' – that sets them apart from their rivals. For example, a company that owns the key pipelines in a country has a huge economic moat because oil and gas companies need to move their goods and the financial, technical and regulatory barriers to building new pipelines are immense, thus protecting against competition and giving the company pricing power.

To summarize, buy shares across several economic sectors and only buy sector leaders that have a solid track record, a diversified product line sold in many countries and have a high but sustainable payout ratio of profits to shareholders as dividends, that are not exposed to non-linear risk, have a business model your child could understand and indeed will come to understand and that are protected by a 'moat'.

This is only a general overview of how to select high-quality, dividend-paying companies. For those interested in learning more about the technical aspects of choosing and evaluating specific dividend leaders, probably the best book on the topic, and the only one you really need to read, is *The Ultimate Dividend Playbook* by Josh Peters.

8

DRIPing Your Way to a Child Millionaire

The final strategy for forging a Child Millionaire is a version of the all-shares portfolio. Although slightly more complicated to setup, this approach may be the cheapest and most powerful method of all. This technique goes by the name of 'Dividend Re-investment Plan,' also known as 'DRIP' or 'DRP' investing. The name 'DRIP' also reinforces the idea of a slow gradual 'drip feed' of money over time to create substantial wealth. The scenario I laid out in the Introduction of the parents who bought Johnson & Johnson shares in 1980 is an example of DRIP investing.

DRIP investing allows you to automatically purchase individual shares in a company without the need for, or costs of, using a brokerage account (after you setup the plan). DRIPing also allows you to own partial shares, which you can't do with a brokerage account, and often you get a discount on the share price of up to 5% off the market rate, thus earning you an instant return on your money. Furthermore, you can usually make regular or annual purchases in addition to the dividend reinvestments, thus taking maximum advantage of dollar/pound cost averaging. This facility for making additional purchases is known as a 'Stock (or Share) Purchase Plan' or 'SPP'.

Sound too good to be true? Well, there are a couple of downsides to DRIPing. Firstly, because your shares aren't held in a brokerage account you can't sell your shares quite as quickly or as easily as with a broker. This can be a massive benefit, though, if you are the type of person who is prone to panic when the market drops or who likes to fiddle with a portfolio, which can be a very costly thing to do. The second major risk is that you can't own ETFs in this system, so your entire portfolio will comprise shares in individual companies, and thus carry substantially greater risk.

So How Do I DRIP My Way to a Child Millionaire?

Back in the day, all stocks were issued as paper certificates and physically held by owners. In the days of electronic trading and brokerages this has changed, and stocks you own are held by the brokerage 'in trust' on your behalf, so you never see a paper certificate. Yet you can still request a paper certificate for shares you own from any company listed on a stock exchange.

The basics of the DRIP system are as follows:

- You purchase a single share of XYZ Company that offers a DRIP and an SPP.
- You enrol in the DRIP offered by XYZ, usually through the company that XYZ uses to manage its shares, which is called a 'registrar' or 'transfer agent.'
- Your dividends are automatically reinvested by the DRIP, purchasing whole or fractions of shares at no cost to you.
- You make regular contributions to the DRIP to purchase more shares, often at a discount to market price and you track your portfolio via an account from the transfer agent at no cost to you.
- You forge a Child Millionaire.

That's it. And the cost after setting up is zero.

So let me take you through the steps of setting up a DRIP Child Millionaire portfolio in more detail.

Step 1

Select the company you wish to purchase shares in – see the above section on Dividend Aristocrats – and check that they offer a DRIP and an SPP or other share purchase programme. Note that the company *must* offer both a DRIP *and* an SPP to be a contender for the Child Millionaire portfolio. You can usually find this information on the company website under the heading 'Investor Relations.'

Step 2

Open a discount brokerage account or use your existing brokerage account to purchase a *single* share in the company. In doing this you will incur the full commission of $10–30 even if the share only costs $20 or $50.

Step 3

After purchasing a single share in XYZ Company, write a letter to
your brokerage company giving your account details and ask to be
sent a physical share certificate for the share you have purchased.
You may be able to do this online. Either way there will typically be
a charge of about $50. If you want the shares and the subsequent
DRIP portfolio to be in your name then request that your name is
on the share certificate. If you want the DRIP portfolio to be in your
child's name while you retain control then request that the share
certificate is registered in your name 'in trust' for your child. The
wording should be 'John Doe in trust for Johnny Doe' using your
real names of course. (See the section below on ownership and
taxes for more on this).

Step 4

Once the share certificate arrives, check that it is in your name or
your name 'in trust' for your child. If it isn't, use the 'Transfer of
Ownership' section on the back of the share certificate to transfer
the ownership and thus change the name. You may have to go into
your bank branch to get them to verify your signature and have
them sign the back as well.

Step 5

Find out what 'registrar' or 'transfer agent' XYZ Company uses.
Check under 'Investor Relations' on XYZ Company's website for
this information. Here you will also find out whether the company
offers DRIP/SPP investors a discount on share purchases. Transfer
agents specialize in handing the logistics of company share
ownership records, paying of dividends and other tasks. There are
a few major players which include CIBC Mellon, Computershare,
Wells Fargo, etc. Next, find XYZ Company in the list on the transfer
agent's website, download and print off the DRIP form and the
SPP/share purchase plan form, and complete the forms. As an
example, check out Enbridge's website. Clicking on 'Investor
Relations' along the top menu gives you all the information you
need about the DRIP, SPP, transfer agent and the 2% discount on
shares.

Step 6

Mail the share certificate, the completed DRIP and SPP forms, and a
cheque for your first regular contribution or your first bulk share
purchase to the transfer agent. It probably helps to ring up the

transfer agent and ask them how to complete the form for a DRIP and SPP being held 'in trust' for a child, what the minimum SPP contribution is if this isn't on their website ($50 is common), who to make a cheque out to and where to send it. The amount you send should be for more than the value of a single share and at least the minimum requirement for a SPP.

Step 7

Depending on your country, the transfer agent will probably send you an 'Anti-Money Laundering' form of some sort, and possibly some withholding tax forms if the company is based outside of your country. You will need to complete and return these forms before they process your DRIP and SPP. Once this is done you will receive an account statement and you can create an online log-in with the transfer agent so you can track your Child Millionaire Portfolio and view your statements online.

Step 8

Make regular contributions (monthly or quarterly is best) to the SPP by sending a cheque, or if possible a regular bank transfer, to the transfer agent, who will then use it to purchase whole or partial shares from XYZ Company with *no commission charge* and often at a discount as an incentive to invest more.

Step 9

All dividends will be automatically reinvested in shares so you can let the DRIP take care of itself and you will be on your way to a Child Millionaire portfolio. You will be amazed at how the portfolio grows without fees and without tinkering.

Step 10

Repeat the process with shares from other companies you want to add to the Child Millionaire portfolio.

The DRIP and SPP will take care of all reinvestment and dollar/pound cost averaging, and you will never have to pay another penny in fees except if your child sells the shares in the far distant future. At any point in the future the dividend stream can be directed into a bank account as cash instead of being reinvested, providing a regular, tax efficient income.

The total cost to set this up, in addition to the share purchase itself, will be $70–100 to cover the purchase commission ($10–30), the share certificate request ($50) and some envelopes and postage ($10), which are basically one-off costs. It might be useful to keep track of the regular DRIP and SPP purchases in a spreadsheet, in addition to the statements the transfer agent sends you, to make tax filing easier in the future if you ever sell the shares and need to figure out any capital gains.

DRIPing can sound complicated but it's actually very straightforward. If at any point you have questions simply ring up the relevant person at the brokerage, the investor relations department of the company you are buying or the transfer agent.

9

Ownership and Tax

What follows is a *general* discussion of some of the key issues related to ownership and tax, and how they might affect the Child Millionaire portfolio. It is not intended to provide specific advice, nor be even remotely exhaustive of the legalities and what is or isn't possible or smart to do in any given country or circumstance. Each country has its own rules and you will need to look into the specific details of how ownership and tax work in your country and for your specific income and other circumstances. It is vital that the ownership structure of the Child Millionaire portfolio *and* the tax obligations are well understood and setup correctly from the start for your jurisdiction, so you might want to talk to a professional tax advisor and make sure you get this right from the start.

Again, generally it isn't that complicated and dealing with tax should *never* be used as an excuse for inaction.

Ownership – Whose Name Should Be on the Child Millionaire Portfolio?

Generally speaking there are four ways that you might structure the ownership of a Child Millionaire portfolio depending on your jurisdiction and situation. These are:

- In your name.
- In your child's name.
- In an informal trust.
- In a formal trust.

In Your Name

If you set-up the Child Millionaire portfolio in your own name, you will have total control over the portfolio and all investment decisions. You will also be liable for all tax due on dividend income even if the portfolio you setup is for your child. If you are in a higher tax bracket, you may have to pay more tax on the income than you might if the portfolio was in the child's name, though this isn't necessarily the case, depending on where you live. The more tax you pay on income, the less there is to reinvest and the less compounding, so you want to take all legal steps to minimize any tax payable.

Later in life you may be able to 'gift' the portfolio to your child without any hindrances. However it is possible you'd have to liquidate the portfolio to cash, or your tax agency might deem you to have liquidated the portfolio, before transferring it to your child, thus crystallizing capital gains and triggering capital gains tax. Such taxes may be avoidable in some jurisdictions if there is an annual capital gains tax exemption (such as the UK), and/or if you have accrued capital losses to offset the gains, and you stagger the withdrawal and transfer of funds to your child over several years. Paying capital gains tax unnecessarily and then repopulating the portfolio with the same shares prior to the transfer could have serious negative impacts on portfolio growth because of a reduction in the size of the portfolio and the chance that the market may go up while your portfolio is in cash. You will also have to pay fees to sell and repurchase the shares.

In Your Child's Name

In principle it might make sense to set up the portfolio in your child's name right from the start. You will need to check whether children are legally allowed to own ETFs and/or shares in your country, and whether a brokerage account can be opened in your child's name. In the UK and Canada, children generally can't open a brokerage account themselves.

In the case of a DRIP-based portfolio, if allowed by law, having the portfolio in your child's name would mean having your child's name on the share certificate as the owner and having the DRIP and SPP set up in his or her name. You will need to check with the transfer agent whether this is possible as any contribution to the SPP may, by law, have to come from a chequing account owned by the DRIP and SPP account holder. In many jurisdictions, Canada for example, children can't open chequing accounts, and under anti-money laundering laws it might only be possible to setup an SPP if a cheque is issued by the SPP account holder. This basically means that a child can't participate in an SPP, though he or she can still own shares and any dividends can be reinvested via the DRIP. In this case it is probably more sensible to setup the DRIP and SPP using the 'your name in trust for your child's name' strategy, otherwise you (or more precisely, your child) may be unable to contribute to the SPP and thus accumulate more shares.

Another consideration is that shares in your child's name would be very difficult, perhaps almost impossible, to sell until the child can do it themselves at age 18. If you desperately needed the money you may be unable access it. This could of course be viewed as a positive because the portfolio is insulated from parental meddling. However this could be problematic if a company gets into trouble and you want to sell the shares to limit losses. A further consideration is that the portfolio would be owned by the child and, if this is a concern, there is little you could do to stop your child from liquidating the portfolio and blowing all of the money once they are old enough to understand what they have.

In a Formal Trust

Formal trusts can be expensive to set up and they require expert, often expensive, legal advice. However for portfolios of a certain size and with many children they may give a good level of tax mitigation while simultaneously, depending on the structure, giving the parents a varied level of control over the portfolio to place limits on what a child can or can't do. You should speak to an investment lawyer about your options and situation if you think a formal trust might be a good option or if you are considering switching an existing portfolio into a formal trust.

In an Informal Trust

In some jurisdictions, an 'informal trust' may offer a good in-between option, provided it is allowed by your tax authority. Check to see whether the tax authority and brokerages allow for you to hold a brokerage account 'in trust' for your child. Different rules apply in different countries. You will also need to check whether it will be you or your child who will be liable for tax on any dividend income.

In the case of DRIP investing, you may be able to set up a portfolio straight away with a share certificate that has 'your name in trust for your child's name' on it. You should also be able to set up an SPP in the same manner, but if you have questions it is best to phone the transfer agent and ask them how to set up an SPP for a child in trust.

Tax

What follows are simply general principles. I am not a tax expert and each jurisdiction is different so you *must* take the time to understand your circumstances and if necessary seek tax advice. In the case of tax advice, unlike much financial planning advice, expertise is valuable and well worth paying for at the outset.

Regarding tax, the basic rule for the Child Millionaire portfolio is to do all you can to avoid tax legally, through tax shelters or by reducing the tax payable, and then to pay up front any tax owing rather than using tax-deferred pension plans to house the portfolio.

Why Not to Use a Tax-Deferred or Locked-In Pension Scheme

As I've said before, I think it is preferable to pay tax up front than to build up a tax bomb through tax-deferred schemes such as UK stakeholder pensions or Roth IRAs in the US. The reason is that although pension schemes can often be set up for children and the parent may gain a tax benefit from doing so, government regulation puts the pension out of reach until a child is in their 50s or 60s. This may be a good thing from the point of view of protecting the money from being spent frivolously. However, it also limits what can be done with the money and when. This means that the money wouldn't be available for use by your child for setting up a business or paying for higher education or drawing an income earlier in life for what ever reason.

Regarding future tax uncertainty and political risk, in the UK for example, the government has a disturbing track record of changing the rules for private pensions such as when money can be withdrawn, whether lump sums can be taken out and how much, and what types of investments a registered pension can or must hold at maturity. With aging populations and spiralling national debts it's conceivable that government shortfalls could be made up by clawing back money from pensions through further rule changes, punitive withdrawal taxes, generally higher future taxes or other measures. Given the 'political risk,' in my view, having the money accessible and paying tax on it at the most advantageous rate in the present is the best option. The Child Millionaire portfolio should then be transferred, when possible, into a tax-free account. This approach more than compensates for the loss of immediate tax relief or tax refund benefits because you and your child avoid the 'unknown unknowns' of future tax policy and the expensive ticking tax time bomb of a tax-deferred pension. Having the money accessible with tax paid also means that, in a worst-case scenario, a Child Millionaire portfolio could be liquidated and transferred into gold, or farm land, or physically taken out of a country if you or your child decides to emigrate or your country's economy or currency crashes. My preference is for accessibility and direct control but you may have a different view, so assess your situation accordingly.

Who Pays?

Generally speaking, tax on investment income accrues to the owner of the investment. However, with children the rules often change regularly and are more complicated, and very often the income from an investment purchased with money gifted to a child is taxable in the hands of the giver. This means if you start a Child Millionaire portfolio with a $5,000 gift to your child, some, or possibly all, of the income will have to be recorded as your income and you will have to pay tax at your prevailing rate.

As an example of the country-specific nature of tax rules, in the UK as of 2011, income generated from monetary gifts to children from parents is taxable in the parent's name if the income exceeds more than £100 per year per parent. This means that you could start a portfolio with £4,000 (£2,000 from each parent), and if that portfolio earns a 5% dividend yield of £200 (£100 earned on the £2,000 from each parent), no tax will accrue to the parent. Any subsequent 'second generation' money, in other words dividends earned from shares purchased with dividend income from the original investment, does not accrue to the parents. As a child is unlikely to have any other income, payable tax should be zero for quite a few years, perhaps long enough for the portfolio to be eventually sheltered in a tax-free ISA, thus legally avoiding any tax and thus maximizing the return on the portfolio.

Furthermore, cash gifts from certain people, such as grandparents, is taxable only in the child's name, so it makes sense to use monetary gifts for the Child Millionaire portfolio. The same is true in some countries, such as Canada and the UK, with money from government-sponsored baby tax credit schemes. Just be sure to retain documentation about the source of money that goes into the Child Millionaire portfolio in case you have to prove the origins to the tax authority.

To summarize the main principles with respect to tax for the Child Millionaire portfolio:

- Examine your tax rules and see what applies.
- If a tax free account for children is available in your country then seriously consider using that to house the Child Millionaire portfolio.
- Consider the other ownership options and select the one best suited to your circumstances and needs.
- See what amounts and types of money can be given to your child, and when and to whom any tax accrues.
- Always work to avoid tax when legal and/or pay the lowest rate possible. Fortunately, dividends are generally tax advantageous.
- Pay any tax owing up front rather than deferring it into an unknown and potentially portfolio, busting future 'tax bomb.'

Good places to start your research into ownership and tax are listed in the Sources and Resources section at the end of this book under the heading 'Tax'.

10

Teaching Your Child about Investing

One of the great advantages of building a Child Millionaire portfolio is to relieve, or lessen, the future financial burden on your child of being born into a competitive world. Money worries can cause considerable stress and limit the options available to your child for choosing and pursuing a fulfilling life. With a strong Child Millionaire portfolio, gone will be the unsavoury prospect of having to work in soul-destroying, dead-end jobs simply to make ends meets in what will undoubtedly be an even more crowded and competitive 'rat race' than the one we live in. With a portfolio under his or her belt, your child will have more life options – not just those afforded by having access to monetary wealth, but also, and perhaps most importantly, the opportunity to pursue their talents, interests and ambitions in the knowledge that their future financial well-being is secure.

It is important, however, to consider what and how you will teach your child about money and the rules of wealth, investing and ownership as he or she grows up. Learning about money, personal finance and participating in management of his or her Child Millionaire portfolio from the moment he or she can understand it is absolutely vital if you want your child to be responsible for the portfolio rather than squandering it. With the right mentoring, your child could go on to augment the portfolio, develop it and perhaps even turn it into an enduring dynastic portfolio of family money for his or her children.

Learning

One way to involve your child in management of their portfolio is to let him or her participate in researching and selecting stocks or ETFs and tracking the results. This sort of participation will help make the portfolio seem 'real' and will teach the basic, core skills of investing and the importance of investing – owning high-quality dividend-paying companies – versus the dead-end of 'saving.'

When your child receives a cash gift from a grandparent, relative or friend you could deposit the money into the Child Millionaire portfolio account and help your child select and purchase stocks or ETF units with the money. He or she can then track the progress of the stock and experience the real-life emotional ups and downs of the markets, and learn about mastering these emotions. You can also use this opportunity to teach your child about the future value of money, the power of compound interest and how to keep track of the dividend payments, with the goal of learning how investing and ownership generate income.

The Child Allowance/Pocket Money 'Mini' Portfolio

When your child reaches the age of receiving or earning 'allowance' or 'pocket money,' you may consider using one small part of the Child Millionaire portfolio – perhaps one particular stock or ETF holding in the portfolio – as a 'mini' portfolio to 'pay' your child.

This is an excellent way to use money given to your child by relatives. It teaches children about making choices, responsibility, capital preservation and accumulation, delayed gratification and participation. For example, let's say that a portion of the Child Millionaire portfolio comprised of money given to your child by relatives has grown to $5,000 by the time your child is 10 years old. At this point you could begin involving the child in selecting investments. He or she could choose the shares in a company they know, perhaps a video game or toy-maker, a computer company, a popular doughnut maker (Canadians take note) or whatever strikes their fancy. Naturally you can help narrow the field and set the parameters of the 'research' task, and your child can create colourful graphs or you can invent other fun activities to chart the portfolio's progress.

If that portion of the portfolio then yields, say, 5%, this will generate $250 per year. You could stipulate that some portion of the money needs to be reinvested to generate more growth and more income in the future, and discuss and project how this will happen and why it is important for compound growth and a larger future income. The other portion can be withdrawn as spending money or for special purchases, holiday spending or according to whatever rules you establish.

This sort of exercise will give your child a very clear sense of how their portfolio contributes directly to their available spending money. It will teach him or her that there is a finite amount of money and that safeguarding and nurturing the portfolio is important. By involving your child early and often there will be tremendous scope for learning about ownership, good money management and investment habits, not to mention honing mathematical and analytical skills. You will help to instil within your child a powerful set of money management skills that most people are never taught and woefully lack, and that will serve him or her for life.

Afterword

The Value of Your Time and Taking Action

People tend to fail to create financial wealth and security not from a lack of money, though this is the usual excuse offered, but rather from a lack of basic investing knowledge, poor habits and a failure to act. You now have the basic knowledge to get started, even with just $50 a month, so the time for action is now.

The Child Millionaire system and ETF-based portfolio I've described takes no more than a few hours to setup and once it is up and running the time commitment drops to a couple of hours a year for reinvestment of dividends. A bit more time is required to research and select individual stocks if you choose to go down this road. In the case of a DRIP, the setup is more complicated and time-consuming – but still only a weekend's work – but once it is up and running the reinvestment takes care of itself, costs nothing and all you have to do is mail a cheque a couple of times a year or, if the transfer agent allows, setup a monthly bank transfer. That's it.

When measured in future value to your child, assume that setting up the Child Millionaire portfolio takes two days in total, 16 hours, once all is said and done. On-going management might amount to four hours a year, perhaps a bit more if you enjoy it and your children get deeply involved. By the time your child is 18 years old you will have invested around 160 hours in the Child Millionaire portfolio, which is about one working day a year. Consider this in light of how much time you might spend watching TV over 18 years.

If you start the portfolio with $1,000 and contribute $100 a month for 18 years, and the portfolio yields 5% with dividend growth of 8% per annum and appreciation of the shares at the rate of inflation of 3%, when you hand it over to your child it will be worth about $75,800. This amounts to getting paid $474 for every hour you 'work' on the portfolio. Where else would you earn $474 per hour? When your child is 40, and if he or she has maintained the modest $100 per month contribution, the portfolio would be worth $11.3 million. In other words your 160 hours spent over 18 years would have been worth over $70,000 *per hour* to your child, and perhaps at this point also to your grandchildren.

Can you in all good conscience afford not to act this very minute? 'I'll do it tomorrow' will, before you know it, turn into a lifetime of regret. You have the knowledge, now action is the only thing you need. Get to it and happy investing!

Resources

High quality information is the lifeblood of investing but too much of the wrong kind can sap your motivation and unnecessarily complicate investment decisions. Below is a short list of useful resources to help build your Child Millionaire portfolio, not intended as an excuse for reading instead of taking action.

Dividend Investing

Websites

www.childmillionaire.com (investing for children)
www.fool.co.uk (dividend investing – UK site)
www.fool.com (dividend investing – US site)
www.seekingalpha.com
http://www.dripprimer.ca/ (Canadian DRIP investing)

Books

Josh Peters, *The Ultimate Dividend Playbook: Income, Insights and Independence for Today's Investor*, John Wiley and Sons, Inc. 2008

If you want detailed methods for evaluating and selecting individual dividend paying companies with rising dividends then look no further than Peters.

Tax

USA

Internal Revenue Service: http://www.irs.gov/

UK

HM Revenue and Customs: http://www.hmrc.gov.uk/index.htm

DirectGov explains the basics of tax liabilities for investment income earned by children
http://www.direct.gov.uk/en/index.htm

Canada

Canadian Revenue Agency http://www.cra-arc.gc.ca/menu-eng.html

Printed in Great Britain
by Amazon